Rooted in the Word

A Lutheran View of the Life of Faith

Ruth Aarhus Vallevik

Rooted in the Word
by Ruth Aarhus Vallevik

Printed in the United States of America

ISBN 9781626972711

www.xulonpress.com

Contents

Dedication

To my parents, Rev. Joseph and Alice Aarhus
Who made it easy to believe in a Heavenly Father's goodness and love

Among my mother's many gifts to me was the wealth of memorized Scripture that is stored in my heart, which brings blessing and comfort even in the hours of the night. Her verbal witness of her faith and her vibrant prayer life impressed me deeply. My father's great gift to me was his example of a daily life of devotion, godliness, conviction and gentle love. His walk matched his pulpit talk, and his daughter noticed.

To my husband, Rev. Bruce Vallevik
My companion, friend and great love for thirty-four years, whom God brought home to Himself in 2005

Bruce taught me to laugh whether days were bright or dark, to love theology, and to serve the Lord with passion and conviction. His life as shepherd, counselor and teacher made an eternal impact on many, many people, and his passing left a hole in my life that will always be unfilled, yet keeps my eyes looking up with a daily longing for reunion on the other side.

And to my children
Kari Vallevik (Scott) McFarland
Jared (Brynde) Vallevik
Whose lives have filled me with joy and pride, and whose acts of lovingkindness and support have brought me immeasurable comfort and hope even on the darkest of days.

Why this book?

Why do we say the Bible is a "means of grace?"
Do Lutherans believe people can "lose" their salvation?
Why are infants baptized?
What does the Bible teach about Christ's return to earth?
What is the "prosperity gospel" and why does it matter?
What is an "emergent" church?
Do Christians still sin?

> "I have watched with growing disbelief as the evangelical church has cheerfully plunged into astounding theological illiteracy...The effects of this great change in the evangelical soul are evident in every incoming class in the seminaries, in most publications, in the great majority of churches, and in most of their pastors."[1]
> - David Wells

This book originated in response to questions from women's groups who are using Bible studies from a wide range of Protestant theological traditions or streams. These studies are written by godly teachers of the Word, but sometimes there is confusion at points of disagreement among evangelicals. Women could fill a bookshelf-lined room in their homes with volumes on these topics, and spend every evening of the next ten years studying them, or we could provide a tool, easily-accessible and understandable, for their ready reference. Though Biblical teaching is often profound and full of mystery because it is the Word of God Himself, far beyond our powers to explain, it doesn't need to be couched in dense and difficult terms, understandable only to the professional theologian. Jesus Himself taught both the masses of ordinary people and individuals from scholarly Nicodemus to Peter the fisherman and zealot.

Rather than pages of text, you will find lists, charts and summaries, as well as references for more extensive study if you desire that. There is also an extensive glossary of terms, as well as lists of people you should know—from church fathers and martyrs to reformers and missionary pioneers. Because I write as a Lutheran and as a member of a small denomination among the many Lutherans, you will find specific references to that church, the Church of the Lutheran Brethren of America. A Lutheran point of view is in many ways the most basic point of view in the Protestant faith. Lutherans were the first "evangelicals." They were a reformation and renewal movement which sought to relate all teaching to the central doctrine of the Gospel, so in many ways the Lutheran point of view is common ground for all people of evangelical faith. This awareness of substantial common ground accounts for my use of many non-Lutheran sources who state a concept or point of view that is appropriate to my purposes and helps make clear this common ground.

Your pastor is your primary resource, of course, as he has the formal theological training that I do not. He will welcome your questions, pray with you for discernment, and support your efforts to reach people with the Gospel.

I wish to express special thanks to the following people who reviewed the manuscript and offered many helpful insights: Dr. Gene Boe, Rev. Rick Bridston, Rev. Omar Gjerness, Rev. John Kilde, Rev. Matthew Lundgren, Rev. Robert M. Overgaard, Sr., and Dr. Ken Peeders. My thanks also to Marcia Bridston and Cheryl Olsen for their careful editing assistance.

A few notes about the format:

- Boxes labeled "This is most certainly true" contain passages from *Explanation of Luther's Small Catechism. (*see Bibliography*)*
- "For further reading": These resources are included for broader study of the topics. Their inclusion does not imply total agreement, but they will contribute to a better understanding of the issues and different viewpoints.

What is Theology?

Theology basically means the study of God and all His works. The term comes from the Greek *theos*, meaning "God," and *logos*, meaning "word" or "discourse", so we have a "discourse" or "study of God."

"Doctrine" is a narrower term. It is what the whole Bible teaches about a particular topic, such as the "doctrine of the Trinity", or the "doctrine of sin."

Five Ingredients Defining Theology: Millard Erickson identifies these as:

- Biblical—using proper methods of biblical research.
- Systematic—studying the whole Bible, relating all parts to each other.
- Relevant—to culture and learning, drawing from other areas of study such as philosophy.
- Contemporary—relating truth to current challenges and questions.
- Practical—not just stating truth, but applying it to life situations. [2]

Fields of Theology: Professor Omar Gjerness describes these as:

<u>Exegetical</u>—which deals with the interpretation of Scriptures, including Hermeneutics, the science or method of biblical interpretation.

<u>Historical</u>—such as Old Testament theology, church history, or missions history. The development of theological understanding through the early centuries of the church.

<u>Practical</u>—The teaching of the Word relating to practical issues of evangelism, counseling, issues in ministry, etc.

<u>Systematic</u>—the collective understanding of what the Bible teaches about various topics.[3]

There are other related studies, such as apologetics (defense of the faith), and ethics (the study of moral behavior— essentially, what is right and wrong). Various theologians also classify the fields of theology in different but similar ways.

The "ologies"

Ecclesiology—the doctrine of the church
Eschatology—the doctrine of last things, end times
Soteriology—the doctrine of salvation
Anthropology—the nature of man
Christology—the nature of Christ
Angelology—the doctrine of angels/Satan/demons
Pneumatology—the doctrine of the Holy Spirit
Theology proper—the doctrine of God
Bibliology—the doctrine of the Bible

"The modern Christian tends to ignore or decry the importance of right doctrine. Tired of endless disputes, Christians today embrace the idea that what really matters is right relationship, not right doctrine. The idea that one is more important than the other is a faulty premise."

- R. C. Sproul[4]

"Correct doctrine in itself is not enough; it is tragically possible to fail to work God's truth out in practical obedience...If correct doctrine does not lead to holy, loving, mature lives, something has gone terribly wrong. But that is no reason for neglecting or discounting it."
- B. Milne[5]

"A church that takes doctrine seriously is a church that is obedient to and responsible for what God has entrusted to it. Doctrine gives substance and weight to what the Christian church has to offer to the world. A church that despises or neglects doctrine comes perilously close to losing its reason for existence and may simply lapse into a comfortable conformity with the world—or whatever part of the world it happens to feel most at home with. Its agenda is set by the world; its presuppositions are influenced by the world; its outlook mirrors that of the world. There are few more pathetic sights than a church wandering aimlessly from one 'meaningful' issue to another in a desperate search for relevance in the eyes of the world."[6]

Endnotes:

---

1. David Wells, "No Place for Truth" cited by Brad Harper of Multnomah Bible College in lecture notes, 2001
2. Millard Erickson, *Christian Theology*, 3 vols. (Grand Rapids: Baker, 1983), 121.
3. Omar Gjerness, *Knowing Good From Evil: A Study in Ethics* (Fergus Falls, Minnesota: Faith & Fellowship Press, 1982), 6.
4. R. C. Sproul, *The Soul's Quest for God: Satisfying the Hunger for Spiritual Communion with God* (Wheaton, IL: Tyndale, 1992), 47.
5. B. Milne, *Knowing the Truth: A Handbook of Christian Belief (*Downer's Grove, IL: Inter-Varsity, 1982), 12.
6. Alister E. McGrath, "Doctrine and Ethics", gen. ed. David Horton, *The Portable Seminary* (Bloomington, MN: Bethany House, 2006), 618.

Chapter 1

Essential Doctrine: What it Means to be a Christian

Essential Doctrines: What It Means to be A Christian

If you don't attend _______ church you are not really saved.
If you don't baptize the way _______ church does you deny the Bible.
The Bible is the truth for me, but it may not be for you.
Jesus Christ was really God who only appeared to be human.
God is only one being who shows Himself in three ways.
The Holy Spirit is not in you if you don't speak in tongues.

Have you ever heard people say these things? Have you ever examined the reasons for the truths that you base your faith upon?

What are the ***core, foundational teachings*** that one must accept and believe in order to be a true Christian? There are many different views of some areas of Christianity, and many different practices from one culture, one age, or one denomination to another throughout history, but on what basic essential truths must they be in total agreement? What should our attitude be towards those of different views?

A familiar phrase, commonly repeated and attributed both to Augustine and to Rupertus Meldenius in 1627 is,

In essentials, unity; in non-essentials, liberty,
and in all things, charity.

The "***essential truths***" of Christianity relate to God the Father, Jesus Christ His Son, the Holy Spirit, the relationship between them that we call the Trinity, and the nature of the Word of God. We could also include the doctrines related to the fallen nature of man, the doctrine of sin and the necessity of salvation. We will deal with the first five here, since the others are presented in separate sections of this book.

"The one thing I am here to say to you is this: that it is worse than useless for Christians to talk about the importance of Christian morality, unless they are prepared to take their stand upon the fundamentals of Christian theology. It is a lie to say that dogma does not matter; it matters enormously. It is fatal to let people suppose that Christianity is only a mode of feelings; it is virtually necessary to insist that it is first and foremost a rational explanation of the universe. It is hopeless to offer Christianity as a vaguely idealistic aspiration of a simple and consoling kind; it is, on the contrary, a hard, tough, exacting and complex doctrine, steeped in a drastic and uncompromising realism." [1]
Dorothy Sayers

The Word of God

Before we can talk of the truths about God, we must first establish the truthfulness of God's message to us— the Word of God, the Bible. Is it totally true in all respects, or is it simply a book which contains God's word to us? Does it contain error or myths about science and history? Can some teachings within it be viewed as true only of an ancient culture and not true in the 21st century?

Historically the evangelical church has held to an **inerrant** Bible. That is, it is totally free from error. It is totally dependable as a foundation for faith in God and for the salvation which He has provided through Jesus Christ.

II Timothy 3:16: "All Scripture is God-breathed and is useful for teaching, rebuking, correcting and training in righteousness so that the man of God may be thoroughly equipped for every good work."

I Corinthians 2:13: *"This is what we speak, not in words taught us by human wisdom but in words taught by the Spirit, expressing spiritual truths in spiritual words."*

The Statement of Faith of the Church of the Lutheran Brethren describes it in this way in paragraph A:

> *The Bible, including both Old and New Testaments as originally given, is the verbally and plenarily (meaning "complete, or "full") inspired Word of God and is free from error in the whole and in the part, and is therefore the final authoritative guide for faith and conduct.*

This is most certainly true….

9. What is the main truth of the Bible?

The main truth of the Bible is that Jesus is the only way of salvation. (John 14:6; Luke 24:45-49)

10. What are the two main teachings of the Bible?

The two main teachings of the Bible are the Law and the Gospel.

11. What is the Law?

The Law is that teaching of the Word of God which tells me how I am to be and what I am to do and not to do. (Leviticus 19:2b)

12. What is the Gospel?

The Gospel is the good news in which God tells me what He has done for me through Jesus Christ, especially in dying for my sin and rising in victory over death and Satan. (I Corinthians 15:1-5)

The Law of God

- God gave us ***three kinds of law*** in the Bible: the ceremonial law, the civil law, and the moral law. The ceremonial and civil laws related to the Hebrew people of the Old Testament and no longer are binding on believers. The moral law, shown in our conscience (Romans 2:15) and in the Ten Commandments (Exodus 20:1-17) is still in effect. (Ephesians 2:14-18; Romans 2;15, Exodus 20:1-17.)
- There are ***three uses of the law*** of God: the political use which enables people to live together in community; the theological use, which shows us our sinfulness and drives us to Christ; the instructive use, which teaches us how to conduct ourselves. All three function at the same time.

"One thing, and only one thing, is necessary for Christian life, righteousness, and freedom. That one thing is the most holy Word of God, the gospel of Christ."

-Martin Luther

Sometimes we hear that Christians should only be reminded of God's grace, and certainly God's grace is the reality to which we cling: the unmerited favor of God that provided a way for us to be saved and to continue to follow in His ways. We would have absolutely nothing—no spiritual life, no hope, no purpose, no power for service—outside of the "amazing" grace of our wonderful God.

But do believers still need to hear about God's law? Dr. Tim Ysteboe, in *We Believe*, answers this way:

"The normal Christian life is characterized by repentance and faith. All persons, believer and unbeliever alike, need to hear the Law [God telling us what we should do and shouldn't do] and the Gospel [God telling us what He has done and what He promises to do.] The believer needs to hear the Law so that smugness and indifference do not crowd out Christ. The unbeliever needs to hear the Gospel since it is the power of God for the salvation of those who believe...When calling for a response from people at the conclusion of the hearing of the Word, the preacher remembers that both believer and unbeliever may have been brought to conviction of sin and sinfulness and need to hear the word of pardon. Therefore, the response for some may be a first time reception of Christ as Savior, for others, it may be a new revelation of God, for others it may be a new awakening to a new area of personal sin. Some may see themselves as prodigals who need to return to the Father's house. Some may see their need to open up their life to Christ in a new way. Each respondent is hearing the Spirit of God convict of sin and point to Jesus through the Law and Gospel." (p. 108-9)

The Structure of the Bible

- The Bible consists of 66 books, written by forty authors inspired by the Holy Spirit of God over a period of about 1600 years.
- There are 39 books in the Old Testament, and 27 in the New Testament.
- These books are called the "canon" (meaning "yardstick") and their selection to be included in the Bible was carefully considered in the very early days of the church because they "measured up."
- The Roman Catholic Church includes a collection of books called the Apocrypha which are not accepted by the Protestant church.
- The books of the Bible may be divided in this way:

1. **Law:** (Pentateuch): Genesis to Deuteronomy
2. **History:** Joshua to Esther
2. **Poetry**: Job, Psalms, Proverbs, Ecclesiastes, Song of Solomon
4. **Prophecy**: Isaiah through Malachi
    5 Major Prophets: Isaiah through Daniel
    12 Minor Prophets: Hosea through Malachi
5. **Gospels**: Mathew, Mark, Luke, John
6. **Acts**: History of the early church
7. **Paul's Letters to the churches:** (epistles) Romans through 2 Thessalonians
8. **Paul's Letters to friends:** I and 2 Timothy; Titus, Philemon
9. **General letters:** Hebrews through Jude
10. **Prophecy:** Revelation

Four Words to Help You Understand Bible Structure

> "If you believe what you like in the gospels, and reject what you don't like, it is not the gospel you believe, but yourself."[3]
> - Augustine of Hippo

Preparation In the Old Testament God makes ready for the coming of the Messiah.

Manifestation In the four Gospels Christ enters the world, dies for the world, and founds His church.

Appropriation In the Acts and the Epistles the ways are revealed in which the Lord Jesus was received, appropriated and applied in individual lives.

Consummation In the book of Revelation the outcome of God's perfect plan is revealed.

Dr. William H. Griffith[2]

Lutherans believe that the Bible is the only source of faith and doctrine; all other revelation is subject to it. Therefore it is of greatest importance that the believer read the Word, studying it carefully and diligently for himself, as well as hearing it preached. Some necessary steps in understanding—or interpreting the Bible are:

1. **Exegesis** (a Greek word meaning 'drawing out" or 'exposing".). The student of the Word first learns what the passage is literally saying, rather than coming to it with a preconceived view about its meaning.
2. **Integration.** What does the passage mean? How does it relate to the context as well as to other Bible passages about the same subject, since the Word does not disagree with itself?
3. **Application.** How does this passage affect my knowledge as well as my actions and behavior? The true test of one's faith is not so much his knowledge of it, but his obedience to it—trusting what it declares, resting on what it promises and obeying what it calls us to do.

The Doctrine of God, the Father

The second essential doctrine about which there must be agreement among true believers is the doctrine of God. Who is He? What are His attributes? How can He be known?

This is most certainly true….

The First Article of the Creed: I believe in God, the Father Almighty, Maker of heaven and earth.
What does this mean?

I believe that God has created me and all that exists. He has given to me and still sustains my body and soul, my senses and all my members, my reason and all the powers of my soul. I believe that He gives me food and clothing, home and family, and all material blessings; that He daily provides abundantly for all the needs of my life, protects me from all danger, and guards and keeps me from all evil. I believe that He does this because of His fatherly and divine goodness and mercy, without any merit or worthiness in me. For all this I should thank, praise, serve, and obey Him. This is most certainly true. *-Explanation of Luther's Small Catechism*

The attributes—or characteristics— of God can be grouped by those which are "*incommunicable*" - those unique only to God (for example, God has always existed, but we have not) and those which are "*communicable*" - those God shares with us or which we may experience in a limited way (for example, God is love, and we are also able to love.)

Dr. Wayne Grudem, in *Systematic Theology*, lists God's incommunicable attributes as:

Independence: "God does not need us or the rest of creation for anything, yet we and the rest of creation can glorify him and bring him joy. This attribute is sometimes called his 'self-existence.' " (Acts 17:24-25; Job 41:11; Psalm 50:10-12; Revelation 4:11)

Unchangeableness: "God is unchanging in his being, perfections, purposes, and promises, yet God does act and feel emotions, and he acts and feels differently in response to different situations. This attribute is sometimes called 'immutability.' " (Psalm 102:25-27 ; James 1:17; Psalm 33;11; Isaiah 46:9-11). Grudem notes that the four words ("being, perfections, purposes, and promises") are taken from Louis Berkhof, *Systematic Theology (*Grand Rapids: Eerdmans, 1939, 1941), p. 58.

Eternity: "God has no beginning, end, or succession of moments in his own being, and he sees all time equally vividly, yet God sees events in time and acts in time, sometimes called God's 'infinity.' " (Ps. 90:2; Revelation1:8, 4:8; John 8:58; Exodus 3:14; Genesis 1:1, John 1:3, I Corinthians 8:6; Colossians 1:16; Hebrews 1:2)

Omnipresence: "God does not have size or spatial dimensions and is present at every point of space with his whole being, yet God acts differently in different places."
(Deut. 10:14; Jeremiah 23:23-24; Psalm 139:7-10; I Kings 8:27)

Unity: "God is not divided into parts, yet we see different attributes of God emphasized at different times. He is the same God always, and everything he says or does is fully consistent with all his attributes.[4]

Dr. Grudem continues by listing God's "communicable" attributes as:

A. Attributes Describing God's Being:
1. Spirituality 2. Invisibility
B. Mental Attributes:
3. Knowledge (God is Omniscient) 4. Wisdom 5. Truthfulness (Faithfulness)
C. Moral Attributes
6. Goodness 7. Love 8. Mercy (Grace, Patience) 9. Holiness
10. Peace (or Order) 11. Righteousness (or Justice) 12. Jealousy
13. Wrath
D. Attributes of Purpose:
14. Will 15. Freedom 16. Power, or Sovereignty (God is Omnipotent)
E. "Summary" Attributes:
17. Perfection 18. Blessedness 19. Beauty 20. Glory [5]

The full explanation of these communicable attributes covers forty pages in Dr. Grudem's text and is truthfully worth the price of the book. The richness of meaning in the character and attributes of our God moves us to deep and joyful praise! Denying any of them would in my view be heresy, disregarding the essentials of Biblical truth.

Names of God

- **Elohim** A Hebrew name for God that emphasizes His strength, power, and superiority over all so-called gods.
- **Adonai** A Hebrew name for God meaning "Lord," or "Master," stressing the lordship or authority of God.
- **Yahweh** The four Hebrew letter YHWH which constituted the name of God often pronounced or written as Yahweh or Jehovah.
- **El Shaddai** God Almighty, the power or strength of God. (Genesis 17:1)
- **El Elyon** God Most High, His supremacy above all gods. (Genesis 14)
- **El Olam** Everlasting God, His unchanging character. (Genesis 21:33)
- **Jehovah-Jireh** "The LORD will provide." (Genesis 22:14)
- **Jehovah-Nissi** "The LORD our banner." (Exodus 17:15)
- **Jehovah-Shalom** "The LORD is peace." (Judges 6:24)
- **Jehovah-Sabbaoth** "The LORD of hosts." (I Samuel 1:3)
- **Jehovah-Maccaddeshcem** "The LORD Thy Sanctifier." (Exodus 31:13)
- **Jehovah-Tsidkenu** "The LORD Our Righteousness." (Jeremiah 23:6) [6]

Immortal, Invisible, God Only Wise
Walter Chalmers Smith (1867); traditional Welsh melody

Immortal, invisible, God only wise, In light inaccessible hid from our eyes.
Most blessed, most glorious, the ancient of Days,
Almighty, victorious—Thy great name we praise.

To all, life Thou givest—to both great and small; In all life Thou livest—the true life of all.
Thy wisdom so boundless, Thy mercy so free,
Eternal Thy goodness for naught changeth Thee.

Great Father of glory, pure Father of light, Thine angels adore Thee, all veiling their sight;
All praise we would render—O help us to see
'Tis only the splendor of light hideth Thee!

The Doctrine of Jesus Christ, Son of God

The third of the essential truths concerns Jesus Christ. Who is He? What are His attributes and what is His work?

This is most certainly true…

The Second Article of the Creed:

I believe in Jesus Christ, His only Son, our Lord, who was conceived by the Holy Spirit, born of the Virgin Mary, suffered under Pontius Pilate, was crucified, dead, and buried; He descended into hell; the third day He rose again from the dead; He ascended into heaven, and is seated at the right hand of God the Father Almighty, from whence He shall come to judge the living and the dead.

Explanation of Luther's Small Catechism

***Second Article of the Creed**, continued*:
What does this mean?
I believe that Jesus Christ, true God, begotten of the Father from eternity, and also true man, born of the Virgin Mary, is my Lord, who has redeemed me, a lost and condemned creature, bought and freed me from all sins, from death, and from the power of the devil—not with silver and gold, but with His holy and precious blood, and with His innocent sufferings and death—in order that I might be His own, live under Him in His Kingdom, and serve Him in everlasting righteousness, innocence, and blessedness; even as He is risen from the dead, and lives and reigns to all eternity. This is most certainly true.

159. Who is Jesus Christ?
Jesus Christ is true God, begotten of the Father, and therefore without beginning, and true man, born of the Virgin Mary. (*John 1:1,14; Matthew 1:21*)

160. Does Jesus then have both a human and a divine nature?
Yes, Jesus has a divine nature from God, the Father from eternity; the human nature He took on Himself from His mother, Mary. (*Matthew 1:18-23; Colossians 2:9)*

162. Why was it necessary for our Savior to be true man?
It was necessary for our Savior to be true man in order that He might fulfill the law for us, and suffer and die in our place. (*Galatians 4:4,5; Romans 5:19; I Timothy 2:5-6*)

163. Why was it necessary for our Savior to be true God?
It was necessary for our Savior to be true God so that His blood might have unlimited power to pay for the sins of all people. (*Hebrews 9:12)*

Explanation of Luther's Small Catechism

The Names of Jesus:

- **God.** This name is given to Him in a number of places in the Bible. Among them:
  John 20:28: Thomas confessed, "My Lord and my God."
  Titus 2:13: Jesus is referred to as "our great God and Savior, Jesus Christ."
  John 1:18: John states that Jesus is "the only begotten God."
- **Lord** ("master;" title of respect, honor, reverence) [7]
  Matthew 22:44: Jesus reminded people that David called Messiah "my Lord."
  Romans 10:9-13: Paul calls Jesus "Lord."
  Hebrews 1:10 applies Psalm 102:25 to Christ, referring to Him as "Lord."
- **Son of God**
  John 5:25: Jesus refers to Himself as the Son of God.
  John 5:18: The Jews understood that He was "making Himself equal with God."
- **The Son of Man**
  Jesus used this title for Himself eighty-four times in the four gospels (Matthew 16:13, Luke 9:18) and it was also used by Stephen in Acts 7:56.
- **The Son of David**
  Matthew 1:1: indicating He was a descendant of King David.
- **Jesus**
  Matthew 1:21: From the Old Testament name Joshua, which means "Yahweh saves."

The "Offices" or "Positions" of Jesus:

Prophet—God spoke through Him to mankind.
Priest— He represents mankind before God.
King—He would come from the tribe of Judah and reign as King forever. (see Psalm 2:6; Isaiah 9:6-7; Daniel 7:13-14; Matthew 22:41-46 and many other references.)

The Attributes of Jesus

These would be the same as the attributes of God the Father previously listed, because He ***IS TRULY God***. This is a simplified list of His attributes:

Eternal—having had no beginning and no end. (John 1:1)
Omnipresent—present everywhere, in every place. (Matthew 28:20)
Omniscient—all-knowing. (John 2:25; John 4:18)
Omnipotent—all-powerful. (Matthew 28:18)
Immutable—unchanging; always the same. (Hebrews 13:8)
Self-existent—He has life in Himself. (John 1:4; 14:6)

His works:
Creator—(John 1:3) Note that Jesus is called the "Word."
Sustainer—Colossians 1:17
Forgiver of sin—(Mark 2:1-12; Isaiah 43:25)
Miracle worker—(see below for list of some miracles which indicate His deity.)

His present work:
Building up the church as "head of the Church."
Interceding for believers. [8]

Signs of the Deity of Christ

The Gospel of John is often recommended to new believers as the place to begin their study of Jesus. It is sometimes called the "book of 7's" because of the claims to Jesus' deity that are shown in seven miracles, seven "I Am's," seven titles, and seven witnesses.

Seven Miracles
- 2:1-11 Turning water to wine
- 4:46-54 Curing the nobleman's son
- 5:1-18 Curing of the paralytic
- 6:6-13 Feeding of the multitude
- 6:16-21 Walking on the water
- 9:1-7 Giving sight to the blind man
- 11:1-45 Raising of Lazarus from death

Seven Titles for Jesus
- 1:1 The Word
- 1:29 Lamb of God
- 1:41 The Messiah
- 1:49 Son of God
- 1:49 King of Israel
- 4:42 Savior of the World
- 20:28 Lord and ...God

Seven "I AM" claims by Jesus Himself
- 6:35 Bread of Life
- 8:12 Light of the World
- 10:7,9,11,14 The Door and the Good Shepherd
- 11:25 The Resurrection and the Life
- 14:6 The Way, the Truth, and the Life
- 15:1,5 The True Vine
- 8:58 The "I AM" (Yahweh of the OT)

Seven Witnesses who declared Him to be God:
- 1:15 John the Baptist
- 1:49 Nathanael
- 6:69 Peter
- 11:27 Martha
- 20:28 Thomas
- 21:24 John the Apostle
- 4:24, 26; 8:24, 28, 58 13:19 Jesus Himself

Eight Essential Truths about Jesus
that one must believe in order to be a true Christian:

1. **Virgin birth of Christ.** He has to be both truly man and truly God in order to save us. He had to have no inherited sinful nature. This supernatural miracle fulfilled the prophecy of Isaiah 7:14. The doctrine, called the "incarnation" means simply that Christ was God "in the flesh." He is fully God and fully man. *(Matthew 1:18-23)*
2. **Sinlessness of Christ.** He had to be sinless in order to make atonement for *our sins*, since He had none of His own to die for. He was born of a virgin and thus had no inherited sin nature, but He also committed no sin in His life on earth. *(2 Corinthians 5:21; Hebrews 4;15; I Peter 2:22)*
3. **Deity of Christ**. He had to be truly and fully God in order to be the perfect mediator between God and man. *(John 1:1; Colossians 2:9; Hebrews 1:8)*
4. **Humanity of Christ**. Jesus needed to be divine in order to save us, and He needed to be human in order to take our place—to represent us. *(John 1:14; Philippians 2:7,8; Hebrews 2:14)*
5. **Atoning Death of Christ.** He had to die in order to pay the price of our sin. *(John 3;16; Mark 10:45; I Peter 2:24; I Peter 3:18; John 14:6)*
6. **Resurrection of Christ**. Christ had to be totally and bodily victorious over death. *(Romans 4:25; Romans 10:9 Luke 24:39)*
7. **Ascension of Christ**. Jesus had to return to the Father to prepare a place for us, to intercede for us, and to leave the Holy Spirit to comfort, teach and guide us. *(John 16:7; Luke 24:50,51; Acts 1:9-10)*
8. **Second coming of Christ**. Jesus promised that He would physically return to earth in the same way He left. He will return to rule and to judge the world. There is a diversity of understanding regarding some details of His return (see section on Eschatology) but we must believe in His promised return. *(Matthew 24:30; Revelation 22:12; Colossians 3:3,4)* [9]

Heresies Concerning Christ

There are three basic heresies concerning Christ which have occurred and re-occurred through the centuries. They are described here by Dr. Wayne Grudem and are more fully described in Chapter 3 of this book, *Twisted Truth: Heresies and False Teaching.*

Apollinarianism. Christ, though one person, had a human body but not a human mind or spirit; the mind and spirit were divine. This view was rejected by the Council of Alexandria in A.D. 362 and the Council of Constantinople in A.D. 381.

Nestorianism. Christ was actually two distinct persons in one body. It was named after Nestorius, a preacher at Antioch who became bishop of Constantinople in A.D. 428. He was removed from his office and his teachings were condemned.

Monophysitism, also called **Eutychianism**. Christ was neither truly God nor truly man but was a mixture of both, resulting in a third kind of nature. [10]

Behold Him there! The risen Lamb, My perfect spotless righteousness;
The great unchangeable I AM—the King of glory and of grace.
One with Himself I cannot die,
My soul is purchased with His blood.
My life is hid with Christ on high, with Christ my Savior and my God,
With Christ my Savior and my God.
- from the hymn "*Before the Throne of God Above*" [11]

The Doctrine of the Holy Spirit

The fourth of the essential truths concerns the Holy Spirit, the third person of the Trinity. Who is He? Is He truly a Person or an Influence? What is His work, and how does He show Himself?

This is most certainly true…

The Third Article of the Creed:

I believe in the Holy Spirit, the holy Christian* church, the communion of saints, the forgiveness of sins, the resurrection of the body, and the life everlasting. Amen. (**some churches use the term "catholic", meaning "universal". Others use "Christian" so as to eliminate confusion with the Roman Catholic Church.)*

What does this mean?

I believe that I cannot by my own reason or strength believe in Jesus Christ, my Lord, or come to Him, but the Holy Spirit has called me through the Gospel, enlightened me with His gifts, and sanctified and preserved me in the true faith, just as He calls, gathers, enlightens, and sanctifies the whole Christian church on earth, and preserves it in union with Jesus Christ in the one true faith, in which Christian church He daily forgives abundantly all my sins, and the sins of all believers, and at the last day will raise up me and all the dead, and will grant everlasting life to me and to all who believe in Christ. This is most certainly true.

207. Who is the Holy Spirit?

The Holy Spirit is the third person of the Trinity and true God with the Father and the Son.

208. What is the work of the Holy Spirit?

The work of the Holy Spirit is to call, gather, enlighten, sanctify, and preserve.

209. How does the Holy Spirit call you?

The Holy Spirit calls me to faith in Christ by the Gospel in Word and Sacraments. (Romans 10:17; 2 Thessalonians 2:14)

211. Why might you not pay attention to the call of the Holy Spirit?

I might not pay attention to the call of the Holy Spirit because 1) The ways of the world are so appealing to me. 2) My human nature desires the ways of the world. 3) I do not appreciate the goodness of God's ways. 4) I want to go my own way. (Isaiah 65:2; 53:6)

212. Why is it dangerous not to pay attention to the call of the Holy Spirit and refuse to come to Jesus?

It is dangerous to do this because I may become hardened so that I no longer desire to come to Jesus nor care whether or not I have His salvation. (Isaiah 55:6,7; Hebrews 3:12,13)

Explanation of Luther's Small Catechism

Dr. Paul Enns, in *The Moody Handbook of Theology,* lists the attributes, work and personhood of the Holy Spirit in this way:

Attributes of the Holy Spirit

He has intellect. (I Corinthians 2:10) "The Spirit searches all things…"

He has knowledge. (I Corinthians 2:11) The Holy Spirit understands the mind of God.

He has mind. (Romans 8:27) The Father knows the "mind" of the Spirit.

He has emotions. (Ephesians 4:30). The Holy Spirit can be "grieved."

He has will. (Acts 16:6) the Holy Spirit redirected Paul's preaching; He also distributes spiritual gifts as He "wills."

Work of the Holy Spirit

He teaches. (John 14:26)
He testifies. (John 15:26)
He guides. (John 16:13)
He convicts. (John 16:8)
He regenerates. (Titus 3:5)
He intercedes. (Romans 8:26)
He commands. (Acts 13:2)
He comforts, or counsels. (John 14:16, 26)

Personhood of the Holy Spirit

He can be **grieved.** (Isaiah 63:10)
He can be **blasphemed.** (Matthew 12:32)
He can be **resisted.** (Acts 7:51)
He can be **lied to.** (Acts 5:3)
He can be **obeyed.** (Acts 10) [12]

Scripture also refers repeatedly to evidence of His deity as a member of the Trinity, as well as divine works in inspiration of Scripture (2 Peter 1:21) and the new birth. (Titus 3:5)

His divine attributes are the same as those of God the Father and God the Son, since the Holy Spirit is ***TRULY GOD***. As stated previously, these include:

Self-existence (Romans 8:2)	**Omniscience** (I Corinthians 2:10-12)
Omnipotence (Job 33:4)	**Omnipresence** (Psalm 139:7-10; John 14:17)
Eternity (Hebrew 9:14)	**Holiness** (Matthew 12:32)
Love (Galatians 5:22)	**Truth** (John 14:17)

The Fruits of the Holy Spirit

The work of the Holy Spirit in the life of the believer becomes evident in certain characteristics or behaviors which are listed in Galatians 5:22-25. It's important to note that these behaviors are not somehow "added on" to the Christian by his own effort, like ornaments placed on a tree to decorate it for Christmas, but are produced by the life of the tree, and that life within is the Holy Spirit Himself. The Holy Spirit leads the Christian to submit to His work, to be sensitive to His correction and leading, to repent and confess sin and to allow him/herself to be cleansed by Him and to produce this "fruit" of the life within. (Philippians 2:13) The writer of Galatians precedes his list of the fruits of the Spirit with a list of "acts of the sinful nature" - a list of truly abhorrent, hideous sinful behaviors, and the contrast is stark.

> ***...But the fruit of the Spirit is:***
> Love, joy, peace, patience, kindness, goodness, faithfulness, gentleness and self-control. Against such things there is no law. Those who belong to Christ Jesus have crucified the sinful nature with its passions and desires. Since we live by the Spirit, let us keep in step with the Spirit..." *-Galatians 5:22-25*

The Gifts of the Holy Spirit

Outside of the understanding of the Trinity, there is hardly another issue of doctrine that so divides many believers as the doctrine of the gifts of the Holy Spirit. To whom are they given? How are they to be used? Are some more important than others? Are they all to be used today? A great revival of interest in the work of the Holy Spirit occurred with the Azusa Street revivals in the early 1900's out of which grew the Pentecostal movement. Again in the 1960's a renewal movement—usually called the Charismatic movement—spread into nearly all denominations throughout the world. We cannot possibly adequately cover the topic here, but will at least list the gifts and the diversity of views of their use in the contemporary church.

Probably the most important thing to remember at the outset is that the Spirit of God does not glorify Himself, but points to Jesus. (John 16:14: "*He will glorify me.*") These gifts that He gives to believers are intended to glorify Christ, to equip the believer for spiritual service, and to bring him to maturity in Christ. They are not the same as natural talents which a person usually has from birth and may be developed, or even transformed and sanctified upon conversion. Instead they are supernaturally given by God, though they, too, need to be recognized, exercised, and developed.

> "The Spirit in a real sense is Jesus' mode of existence now. (Romans 1:4; I Corinthians 15:45; I Timothy 3:16; I Peter 3:18). To experience the Spirit is to experience Jesus. (John 14:16-28; Romans 8:9-10; I Corinthians 6:17; 12:4-6; Ephesians 3:16-19; Revelation 2:3). One cannot know Jesus apart from the Spirit or other than through the Spirit. One cannot experience the Spirit other than this: The Spirit bears the character of Christ and impresses that character on those who submit to it. Any other spiritual experience is to be discounted by the Christian, entirely disregarded and avoided." [13]
>
> -James D. G. Dunn

There are three lists given in the Bible:

Romans 12:6-8 :

Prophesy
Service
Teaching
Encouraging
Giving
Leadership, or Administration
Showing Mercy

I Corinthians 12:8-11:

Wisdom
Knowledge
Faith
Healing
Miracles
Prophecy
Discerning spirits
Speaking in tongues
Interpretation of Tongues

And verse 28 continues:

apostles, prophets, teachers, workers of **miracles,** those having gifts of **healing**, those able to **help** others, those with gifts of **administration,** and those speaking in different kinds of **tongues.**

Ephesians 4:11: "It was He (Christ) who gave some to be **apostles,** some to be **prophets,** some to be **evangelists** and some to be **pastors** and **teachers,** to prepare God's people for works of service, so that the body of Christ may be built up until we all reach unity in the faith and in the knowledge of the Son of God and become mature, attaining to the whole measure of the fullness of Christ."

There are essentially five views regarding the use of spiritual gifts in the church today. These views are explained in the preface to the book, *Are Miraculous Gifts For Today: Four Views.*

1. Cessationist position. There are "no miraculous gifts of the Holy Spirit today. Gifts such as prophecy, tongues, and healing were confined to the first century, and were used at the time the apostles were establishing the churches and the New Testament was not yet complete." This view is held by many evangelicals.

2. Pentecostals (First wave). This refers to any denomination or group that traces its origin back to the Pentecostal revival that began in the United States in 1901 and holds these doctrines: all the gifts of the Spirit are intended for today; baptism in the Holy Spirit is an empowering experience that occurs after conversion; Baptism in the Holy Spirit will result in speaking in tongues as a "sign" that they have received this experience. The Assemblies of God would be an example of this group.

3. Charismatics (Second wave). This refers to groups that trace their origin to the charismatic renewal movement of the 1960's and 1970's, that usually haven't formed denominations but work for renewal within existing ones including both Protestant and Catholic, and that seek to practice all the spiritual gifts mentioned in the New Testament.

4. The Third Wave (so-called by C. Peter Wagner from Fuller Seminary) These groups encourage the equipping of all believers to use the New Testament spiritual gifts today. They believe that "signs, wonders, and miracles" should accompany the presentation of the Gospel, that Baptism in the Spirit happens to all Christians at conversion, but subsequent experiences are better called "fillings" or "empowerings" with the Holy Spirit, and they don't emphasize the gift of tongues as much as Pentecostals and Charismatics do.

5. Open but Cautious. Dr. Grudem adds this view, which he describes as widely accepted among many evangelicals. These Christians "are open to the possibility of miraculous gifts today, but are concerned about the possibility of abuses...they don't think speaking in tongues is ruled out by Scripture, but they see many modern examples as not conforming to scriptural guidelines; some also are concerned that it often leads to divisiveness and negative results in churches today." While they value some of the benefits that these groups have brought to the evangelical world, they would prefer a greater emphasis on evangelism, Bible study and faithful obedience rather than miraculous gifts. [14]

Because of the Lutheran position of "sola scriptura" - the Word alone—most Lutherans would oppose any revelation, view, experience or "enthusiasm" which would not be consistent with the clear written truth of the Word of God.

The Doctrine of the Trinity

Finally, the fifth doctrine essential to all Christians is the doctrine of the Trinity. It has been presented as we have looked at the teaching about God the Father, God the Son and God the Holy Spirit. The word "Trinity" does not appear in Scripture, but the truth of the word clearly does. The concept is virtually impossible for us to fully understand, though many attempts have been made to describe and diagram it. What we know to be true is:

- There is one eternal God and one alone. (Deuteronomy 6:4; John 17:3; I Corinthians 8:4)
- He exists as three persons, Father, Son, and Holy Spirit—each of whom is fully God.

The "persons" are described this way by Dr.Tim Ysteboe in *We Believe*:

"On the basis of Scripture, we think of the three persons as: the Father, who is neither begotten nor sent, but eternally begets the Son and sends the Spirit; the Son, who is begotten from eternity by the Father, of the same essence as the Father and who with the Father sends forth the Spirit; and the Spirit, who is of the same essence as the Father and the Son and who from eternity proceeds from Father and Son and is sent forth by Father and Son. These acts are called the personal acts or the inward operations of the Trinity. They attempt to describe, using biblical terms, the distinctions within the Trinity that address how the three persons relate to each other."[15]

One of the Biblical pictures that displays the three persons of the Trinity at one time in one place (from the human point of view) is at the Baptism of Jesus. Here God the Father speaks, saying "This is my beloved Son in whom I am well pleased." As He speaks, the Holy Spirit in the form of a dove descended on Him. (Luke 3:21-22)

This is most certainly true...

127. Why is God called by Christians, God the Father, God the Son, and God the Holy Spirit?
Because He is One being who has shown Himself to be three persons who are equal.

129. Is God the Father older or more important than God the Son, or God the Holy Spirit?
No, the Three are One, perfectly equal in all things and have always existed.

130. Why is the teaching of the Trinity... so important?
The teaching of the Trinity is so important because it makes known the One True God in whom alone there is salvation. (John 17:3— "Now this is eternal life: that they may know you, the only true God, and Jesus Christ whom you have sent.")

Explanation of Luther's Small Catechism

Historical heresies regarding the Trinity

Most of the heresies that developed in the early church—and that still exist today—concern the truth of the Trinity. They may be summarized as:

- **Tri-theism**. That there are really three Gods, rather than one who exists in three persons. They are only loosely associated.
- **Modalism** (sometimes called Sabellianism). That Father, Son, and Holy Spirit are only three manifestations or "modes of existence" of one God. One God with three "faces."
- **Arianism**. This heresy denied the deity of Christ by placing Him as subordinate to the Father. It understood "begotten" of the Father to mean "created by" the Father, indicating that there was a time in eternity when Christ did not exist.

Dr. Francis Schaeffer in *The Church Before the Watching World* makes the point that doctrines are sometimes seen by certain groups as statements that must be worded exactly in their own way, with no variation whatsoever. All issues are seen in this narrow way, whether they may be deemed essential to salvation or not. Young people rebelling against this sometimes throw everything out, and turn entirely away from Christ. Schaeffer suggests that doctrine could be seen less as a "point" than as a "circle", allowing a degree of freedom of expression. At the same time the edge of the circle is an absolute limit past which we "fall off the edge of the cliff" and are no longer Christians.[16]

We have attempted to define those "edges" in this section - the essential doctrines on which all true believers must agree.

In Summary

Five Cults and Their Views of Essential Doctrines

Adapted from: Geisler. *Essential Doctrine Made Easy* [17]

	Latter Day Saints Mormonism	Jehovah's Witnesses	Scientology	Christian Science	Unification Church (Moonies)
One God	Deny	Accept	Deny	Deny	Redefined
Trinity	Deny	Deny	Deny	Deny	Deny
Human Depravity	Redefine	Accept	Deny	Deny	Redefined
Christ's Virgin Birth	Redefine	Accept	Deny	Deny	Deny
Christ's Sinlessness	Accept	Accept	Deny	Redefine	Deny
Christ's Deity	Deny	Deny	Deny	Deny	Deny
Christ's Humanity	Redefine	Accept	Redefine	Redefine	Accept
Christ's Atoning Death	Redefine	Redefine	Deny	Deny	Deny
Christ's Resurrection	Accept	Deny	Deny	Deny	Deny
Christ's Ascension	Accept	Deny	Deny	Deny	Deny
Christ's Second Coming	Accept	Deny	Deny	Deny	Deny

For further reading and study: There are extensive sections on God the Father, Jesus Christ the Son, the Holy Spirit and the Trinity in each of these texts: Robert Kolb, *The Christian Faith*; Wayne Grudem, *Systematic Theology;* Paul Enns, *The Moody Handbook of Theology;* David Horton, *The Portable Seminary*; Steven P. Mueller, ed. *Called To Believe, A Brief Introduction to Christian Doctrine;* Tim Ysteboe, *We Believe*. Also, Wayne Grudem/Stanley N. Gundry's *Are Miraculous Gifts For Today*; Stanley N. Gundry, *Five Views On Law and Gospel;* Carl F. Wisloff, *I Know In Whom I Believe*. A very useful tool for the understanding and discovery of personal spiritual gifts is *Membership and Ministry Profile* by Mels Carbonell, available from Uniquely You Resources (www.myuy.com)

Endnotes:

---

1. Dorothy Sayers, *Creed or Chaos*? (London: Meuthen, 1947), 28. Quoted in David Horton, gen. ed, *The Portable Seminary* (Bloomington, MN: Bethany House, 2006), 613.
2. William H. Griffith Thomas, quoted in Henrietta C. Mears, *What the Bible is All About* (Glendale, CA: Regal Books, 1979), 346.
3. Augustine of Hippo, quoted in Alister E. McGrath, gen. ed., *Zondervan Handbook of Christian Beliefs* (Grand Rapids: Zondervan, 2005), 27.
4. Wayne Grudem, *Systematic Theology: An Introduction to Biblical Doctrine* (Grand Rapids: Zondervan, 1994), 156-177, 181.
5. Ibid. 185-225.
6. Paul Enns, *The Moody Handbook of Theology* (Chicago: Moody Publishers, 2008), 201.
7. Merrill Unger, *Unger's Bible Dictionary*, 3rd ed. (Chicago: Moody Publishers, 1966), 665.
8. Enns, *The Moody Handbook of Theology*, 237-238.
9. Norman L. Geisler, *Essential Doctrine Made Easy* (Torrance, CA: Rose Publishing, Inc., 2007), pamphlet.
10. Grudem, *Systematic Theology*, 554-555.
11. Cheritie L. Bancroft and Vikki Cook, "Before the Throne of God Above," 1997 PDI Praise.
12. Enns, *The Moody Handbook of Theology*, 258-260.
13. James D. G. Dunn, "The Doctrine of God the Holy Spirit," gen. ed. David Horton, *The Portable Seminary* (Bloomington, MN: Bethany House, 2006), 159.
14. Wayne Grudem, ed., *Are Miraculous Gifts for Today? Four Views* (Grand Rapids: Zondervan, 1996). Counterpoints Series, Stanley N. Gundry, series ed., 10-13.
15. Tim Ysteboe, *We Believe: A Commentary on the Statement of Faith* (Fergus Falls, MN: Faith and Fellowship Press, 2009), 31.
16. Francis A. Schaeffer, *The Church Before the Watching World* (Downers Grove, IL: InterVarsity, 1971), 83-85.
17. Giesler, *Essential Doctrine Made Easy*, pamphlet.

Chapter 2

The Church: The Body of Christ

The Church—The Body of Christ

I just returned from a walk around the blocks near my home. As I reached the adjacent football field I decided it looked like a pleasant shortcut. There were a few small patches of snow, but the sun was shining, the air was crisp and invigorating, and the view off to the hills was inspiring! But in a short while I found the "patches" of snow far deeper and slicker than I expected and—worse yet—I couldn't enjoy the distant view because the deer also had visited this grassy space recently. Avoiding the evidence they'd left required great care at each step! Quite a shortcut!

The point? What can seem to be a clear and obvious path to a goal can—upon closer inspection—be full of pitfalls.

So what does that have to do with church?

You may move to a community, see a church building on the corner that has a cross on top, "Christian" on its sign, a pastor's name and a welcome. It may even have a Bible verse or pithy saying, and may have "Prayer Meeting" on its schedule. Must be a good church, right? Not necessarily so.

Let's inspect a little.

> "The church exists for nothing else but to draw men into Christ, to make them little Christ's. If they are not doing that, all the cathedrals, clergy, missions, sermons, even the Bible itself, are simply a waste of time. God became man for no other purpose."[2]
>
> -C. S. Lewis

What is the Church?

Do you remember the Sunday School song:

A church is not a building, a church is not a steeple,
a church is not a resting place, a church is the people.
And when the people gather there's singing and there's praying,
there's laughing and there's crying sometime—all of it saying:
I am the church! You are the church!
We are the church together!
All who follow Jesus, all around the world,
Yes, we're the church together!

-Richard K. Avery and Donald S. Marsh [1]

The church is people— actually very particular people. It is those who have accepted the truth of the Gospel of Jesus Christ, been saved from their sins and become His children by God's grace alone, through faith alone. They are followers of Christ; they are believers in Him.

We call these people the "church universal", or the "invisible church". It is a body made up of believers in community all across the planet, gathering in homes, shops, caves, under trees, in humble wooden sanctuaries or in vast cathedrals. They may even be in solitude, particularly in countries where believers in Christ are persecuted. They still BELONG!

The church is people.

What about individual congregations?

The church has grown as the Great Commission—Jesus' command to "go and make disciples of all men, baptizing them in the name of the Father and of the

Son and of the Holy Spirit, and teaching them to obey everything I have commanded them," (Matthew 28:18-20) has been carried out. These believers through the ages since Pentecost have grouped themselves within their communities. Sometimes that is by location or by age group, but most often, especially since the division of the Catholic Church in 1054 AD this grouping is by differing understandings of Scripture, by traditional religious practice, by renewal movements, or ethnicity.

Some possible ways of grouping churches today:

- Evangelical/mainline

The primary distinction between them is their view of the inerrancy of Scripture.

Evangelical churches often have broken away from the larger, mainline bodies over that issue. For example, the Presbyterian Church USA (PCUSA) is the mainline church, while the Presbyterian Church in America (PCA) is the more evangelical church.

The Church of the Lutheran Brethren did not break away from any other denomination, but rather grew out of the renewal movement among Lutherans in Norway. For an extensive and enlightening discussion of this highly relevant history, see Rev. Joseph Levang's *Living Lutheran Christianity*, particularly pages 82-119. [3]

- Denominational/non-denominational

Historically most congregations belonged to or were affiliated with a denomination, but there has been a growing movement toward non-affiliation. However, most non-denominational churches in America at present would likely be either Baptist or Pentecostal in their doctrinal positions.

- Liturgical/non-liturgical

Liturgy is the organized structure of worship, printed prayers and responses followed by many more-formal churches. The extent to which it is used varies widely, from the "high" liturgy of the Anglicans to less structured or "low" worship of some Lutheran denominations. Most Protestant churches do have an established order of worship even though it may not include what is commonly understood as liturgy.

Inerrancy is the teaching that all Scripture is given by God and is free from error in all its contents. The doctrinal statement of the Evangelical Theological Society states: "The Bible alone, and the Bible in its entirety, is the Word of God written and is therefore inerrant in the autographs." The Church of the Lutheran Brethren Doctrinal Statement of Faith reads: "The Bible, including both Old and New Testaments as originally given, is the verbally and plenarily *[means "full"]* inspired Word of God and is free from error in the whole and in the part, and is therefore the final authoritative guide for faith and conduct." (Article II A) [4]

"An evangelical is a plain, ordinary Christian. We stand in the mainstream of historic, orthodox, biblical Christianity. So we can recite the Apostles Creed and the Nicene Creed without crossing our fingers. We believe in God the Father and in Jesus Christ and in the Holy Spirit. Having said that, there are two particular things we like to emphasize: the concern for authority on the one hand and salvation on the other. For evangelical people, our authority is the God who has spoken supremely in Jesus Christ. And that is equally true of redemption or salvation. God has acted in and through Jesus Christ for the salvation of sinners." -John R.W. Stott [5]

The Purpose of the Church

Wayne Grudem, in his *Systematic Theology,* describes the purpose of the church:

1. To God, it is *worship.*

Colossians 3:16: "Let the word of Christ dwell in you richly as you teach and admonish one another with all wisdom, and as you sing psalms, hymns and spiritual songs with gratitude in your hearts to God."

2. To believers, it is *nurture.*

Colossians 1:28: "We proclaim him, admonishing and teaching everyone with all wisdom, so that we may present everyone perfect in Christ."

3. To the world, it is *evangelism and mercy.*

Evangelism is the spreading of the good news of Christ's salvation for all, and mercy reflects Jesus' consistent teaching to care for the poor, needy, enemies, and the mistreated.

Grudem carefully explains the necessary balance: "Such ministries of mercy to the world should never become a substitute for genuine evangelism or for the other areas of ministry to God and to believers." [6]

Membership in the Church

"*This is most certainly true*…"

248. Who may be a member of a congregation of Christian people?

Anyone who has been baptized, who confesses faith in Christ as Savior, and who follows the procedures for membership in a particular congregation may be a member.

Explanation of Luther's Small Catechism

Membership in the local congregation is not like joining a club or civic organization. In Lutheran Brethren churches, individuals requesting membership are asked to provide a personal testimony of faith in Jesus Christ as Savior, either written or verbal. That does not guarantee that all members are personal believers, however, as there may be those who state that, but do not truly believe (hypocrites), or who once believed but have now turned from their faith.

Ways of affiliating with a Lutheran Brethren Church

- Parishioner. This term includes all the people who call a particular congregation their church home.
- Baptized Child of the Congregation. These are the children who have been baptized in the congregation as well as those who may have transferred there with their parents. This status continues until they reach the voting age determined by the congregation, or are accepted as confessing members.
- Confessing Member. These are people, above confirmation age, who have requested membership and have been accepted into the congregation. This process sometimes involves attending a membership class, an interview with the Board of Elders and/or pastor, and a vote of the congregation, based on a person's personal confession of faith. It implies a commitment to the congregation's teaching, spiritual guidance and fellowship.

For further study: "*Membership in a Lutheran Brethren Congregation.*" Available from Faith & Fellowship Publishing. www.ffpublishing@clba.org.

Essential Doctrines of the Church

The most basic, fundamental teachings that unite all true believers in Christ center on:

1. The person and work of **God the Father.**
2. The person and work of **Jesus Christ.**
3. The person and work of the **Holy Spirit.**
4. The truth of the **Word of God.**

These essential truths are explained in depth in the first chapter of this book. They are also summarized in several creeds ("statements of belief") of the church, including the Apostles, the Nicene, and the Athanasian . (See Appendix 3) For Lutherans the most familiar is the Apostles Creed, often recited as a part of worship. Note the specific truths that are listed.

I. I believe in God, the Father Almighty, Maker of heaven and earth.

What does this mean?

I believe that God has created me and all that exists. He has given to me and still sustains my body and soul, my senses and all my members, my reason and all the powers of my soul. I believe that he gives me food and clothing, home and family, and all material blessings; that He daily provides abundantly for all the needs of my life, protects me from all danger, and guards and keeps me from all evil. I believe that He does this because of His fatherly and divine goodness and mercy, without any merit or worthiness in me. For all this I should thank, praise, serve, and obey Him. This is most certainly true. [7]

II. I believe in Jesus Christ, His only Son, our Lord, who was conceived by the Holy Spirit, born of the Virgin Mary, suffered under Pontius Pilate, was crucified, dead, and buried; He descended into hell; the third day He rose again from the dead; He ascended into heaven, and is seated at the right hand of God the Father Almighty, from whence He shall come to judge the living and the dead.

What does this mean?

I believe that Jesus Christ, true God, begotten of the Father from eternity, and also true man, born of the Virgin Mary, is my Lord, who has redeemed me, a lost and condemned creature, bought and freed me from all sins, from death, and from the power of the devil—not with silver and gold, but with His holy and precious blood, and with His innocent sufferings and death—in order that I might be His own, live under Him in His Kingdom, and serve Him in everlasting righteousness, innocence, and blessedness; even as He is risen from the dead, and lives and reigns to all eternity. This is most certainly true. [8]

III. I believe in the Holy Spirit, the holy Christian church, the communion of saints, the forgiveness of sins, the resurrection of the body, and the life everlasting. Amen.

What does this mean?

I believe that I cannot by my own reason or strength believe in Jesus Christ, my Lord, or come to Him, but the Holy Spirit has called me through the Gospel, enlightened me with His gifts, and sanctified and preserved me in the true faith, just as He calls, gathers, enlightens, and sanctifies the whole Christian church on earth, and preserves it in union with Jesus Christ in the one true faith, in which Christian church He daily forgives abundantly all my sins, and the sins of all believers, and at the last day will raise up me and all the dead, and will grant everlasting life to me and to all who believe in Christ. This is most certainly true. [9]

Worship in the Church

Elements of worship:

Preaching of the Word	Scripture reading
Prayer	Music
Praise	The Lord's Supper (usually weekly or monthly)

Worship emphasizes the "vertical" dimension of faith. It is first God speaking to us in Word and sacrament and then we speak to Him in confession, thanksgiving, praise and prayer. Often the horizontal dimension of faith, in fellowship with other believers as well as testimony, occurs informally following worship or at other events in the church schedule. It also occurs regularly outside of the church doors!

The Church Year (sometimes called the Liturgical Year)

Worship in churches is often grouped around "seasons" of the year, with different theological and worship emphasis based on periods of the life of Christ. It begins with the four Sundays of Advent**.** (See chart on following page)

Preaching in many churches is organized in a similar way. Pericope texts (also called the Lectionary, and literally meaning "section" or "extract" in the Greek) are assigned to each Sunday: an Epistle text, a Gospel text, and a Lesson. These selections of the Bible are divided over a three-year cycle and used as readings in corporate worship or as the sermon text. The pattern appears to date back to the 4th century.

What does it matter? The purpose of these texts is to direct worship and teaching to the whole of the Bible, and also to ensure that preaching does not over-emphasize one particular topic or ignore others altogether. In an Easter Sunday service at a Lutheran church, for example, you are not likely to hear a topical sermon on marriage. That actually did occur in a church, on the highest celebration day of the entire church year! Lutherans also value **expository** preaching—thoroughly studying, explaining and applying a particular portion of Scripture, rather than "admonishment" preaching, such as "Ten Steps to a Happy Homelife." It's not that the Bible does not have much to say about that subject, but we usually begin with the text, and move to its application.

The Church Year (Liturgical Year)

Advent: means "arrival" or "coming" and is observed the four Sundays before Christmas. It ends on Christmas Eve. Churches often use an "Advent wreath" to mark the Sundays as hope, faith, joy, and love.

Christmas—The twelve days of Christmas begin Christmas Eve and last until Epiphany.

Epiphany (January 6) honors the baptism of Christ, and is also associated with the Nativity, and the visit of the Magi.

"**Ordinary Time**", or "**Time After Epiphany**" These are the Sundays between Epiphany and Lent. Note that "ordinary" does not mean "everyday". It comes from the word "ordinal", meaning the counted weeks.

Lent—The fast of 40 days before Easter, which begins with Ash Wednesday, and was first mentioned in AD 325 as a time for penance, reflection, and focus on Christ's suffering and death.

Passion Week begins with Palm Sunday (the triumphal entry of Jesus to Jerusalem), Maundy Thursday (the Last Supper of Jesus with His disciples), Good Friday (the crucifixion of Jesus), and Holy Saturday.

Easter Sunday—the celebration of Jesus' resurrection from the dead.

Ascension Sunday—40 days after Easter, remembering when Jesus returned to heaven.

Pentecost—celebrates the sending of the Holy Spirit, marking the birth of the church.

"**Ordinary Time After Pentecost**" - extends to Advent

Lutherans also celebrate ***Reformation Sunday***, the Sunday before October 31, commemorating Martin Luther's posting of the 95 Theses on the door of the castle church in Wittenberg, Germany—marking the beginning of the Reformation. [10]

For your information: Holy days in the Jewish calendar:

- ***Pesach*** (Passover)
- ***Shavuot*** (Pentecost)
- ***Yom Kipper*** (Day of Atonement)
- ***Sukkot*** (Tabernacles)
- ***Hanukkah*** (Dedication of Lights)
- ***Purim*** (commemorates the deliverance of the Jews from the Persians) [11]

What's in a Name?

Churches belonging to denominations usually include their affiliation as a part of their name (Our Redeemer's Lutheran Church), while in recent years some have chosen to eliminate that designation. They usually do so to avoid perceived barriers to reaching communities for Christ, thus "Our Redeemer's Church". Others believe that to obscure their identification leads to confusion, noting that certain cults have begun calling themselves "Community Church" or "Fellowship Church."

Non-denominational churches are often given names that include the words "Community" or "Fellowship", or may not use the word "Church" at all: "Community In Christ," "Hosanna," "Celebration!". Though they are not officially linked to a particular denomination, most at present are either Baptist or Pentecostal in doctrinal positions. Visitors are wise to read a church's Statement of Faith, which is usually on their website.

The Church of the Lutheran Brethren incorporates "Lutheran" to describe its doctrinal positions, and "Brethren" to emphasize the "body life" or fellowship of believers within the church. The CLB grew out of the Pietism renewal movement in the State Church of Norway in the later 19th century, reacting to what was viewed as the dead orthodoxy of Lutheranism at that time, a disconnect between belief system and daily lives; between faith and walk.

Church Government

Most Protestant churches are organized under one of three forms of church government, each having its strengths as well as its weaknesses:

Episcopal Presbyterian Congregational

Episcopal:

The Episcopal form of government is hierarchal, i.e., authority moves from the top down. It generally proceeds from archbishop (the highest in authority) to bishop to diocese (churches under the jurisdiction of a bishop) to rector or vicar (an assistant to the rector), who is in charge of the local parish. Archbishops, bishops and rectors are all priests, having all at one time been ordained into the priesthood. It seems clear from church history that this form of government was the major practice in the very early church.

Dr. Tim Ysteboe, in *We Believe,* comments: "The strengths of the Episcopal form of government include simplicity in decision-making, economy of action, and strong oversight of the church. In addition, the local congregation can find help from outside (the bishop) to find resolution to an internal problem. As for weaknesses, 'What if you get a bad bishop?' There is also the potential for a lack of ownership of church mission by the local congregation."[12]

Some denominations that have the Episcopal form of government or variations of it include: Roman Catholic, Orthodox, Episcopal, some Lutherans, some Methodists.

Presbyterian:

The Presbyterian form of church government is more representational, with each local church electing elders to a session. The pastor is one of the elders. The "session" has authority over local congregations. Members of the "session" are also members of the presbytery, which has authority over several regional churches. A general assembly is made up of members of the presbytery and has authority over all Presbyterian churches in the nation or region. The authority, then, is more "bottom up", moving from the local congregation to elected elders, to local session, to regional presbytery, to national general assembly.

Dr. Ysteboe comments: "The strengths of the Presbyterian system are similar to some of the oversight strengths of the Episcopalian system with the added benefits of plurality in leadership. Also, the elders who are making decisions in the church in the Presbyterian system are informed on the issues and in biblical knowledge. The weakness is that decision-making can become slow, and either the presbytery (leadership over a group of congregations) or the local session (leadership of a single congregation), or both, may become isolated and self-perpetuating." [13]

Some denominations that use this system are Presbyterians (several different denominations) and Reformed (also several different groups.)

Congregational:

This form involves the most participation of the lay people of the congregation, and includes at least five different variations:

1. Single-elder (or single-pastor)

The pastor is seen as the only elder in the church and is elected by the congregation.

An elected board of deacons is under his authority, so they serve primarily in an advisory capacity. This form is the most common among Baptist churches.

2. Pastor and plural local elders

Elders, elected by the congregation, govern the church and the pastor is viewed as a teaching/preaching elder—a leader among the elders, having no more authority than they.

3. Corporate Board

Congregations elect a church board, who hire a pastor. The pastor is not seen as a spiritual leader but more as an employee, with the church board being his boss.

4. Pure Democracy

In this form of congregational government there are no elders. Everything is voted on by the members of the congregation, but there is structure.

5. No government but the Holy Spirit

This is actually not an organized form of government at all and is more common in very new churches with more mystical or extreme doctrinal positions. Decisions are made by consensus of the congregation as they feel led by the Holy Spirit in their own personal lives.

According to Dr. Grudem in *Systematic Theology*, "This form of government never lasts very long. Not only is it unfaithful to the New Testament pattern of designated elders with governing authority in the church, but it is also subject to much abuse, because subjective feelings rather than wisdom and reason prevail in the decision-making process." [14]

Some denominations that use various forms of the Congregational system of government include Baptists, Mennonite, Congregational, The Evangelical Free Church, and the Church of the Lutheran Brethren, which uses a congregational system in the synodical organization, but a modified Presbyterian form in the local congregation. Each congregation in the CLB is autonomous in the synod, but governed locally by a board of elders, of whom the pastor serves as the teaching elder.

Dr. Ysteboe, on this form of governance: "A strength of the congregational form of government is involvement in the decision process by those who are going to have to live with the decision. This involvement respects each of God's people and helps them commit to the course they have chosen. The weakness is that people may make decisions without the advantage of good or adequate information." [15]

Officers in the Church

1. **Apostles:** The apostles were unique in that they had to have personally seen Jesus after his resurrection, and had been specifically commissioned by Christ as his apostle. Sometimes the word is used today in a very broad sense of one who has been commissioned or sent. But the biblical model of the office of "apostle" required these two qualifications and therefore is not used for contemporary leaders in the church. (note that the Apostle Paul met the resurrected Christ on the Damascus Road, where he was also called.)
2. **Elders** (also called pastors, overseers, or bishops). This was the NT pattern of leadership. See Acts 14:23, 20:17, Titus 1:5, and two lists of qualifications for elders (I Tim. 3:2-7, and Titus 1:6-9)
3. **Deacons**: The word means "servant" and these people were chosen for tasks related to caring for the members of the congregation. Acts 6:1-6 describes their selection in the early church, and other passages such as I Timothy 3:8-13 and Philippians 1:1 mention them.
4. **Trustees:** This office is not mentioned in the Bible but is an office in many churches Trustees are entrusted with the financial operation of the church as well as the supervision of its property.

Signs of a Healthy Church

Alive! Vibrant! Engaged! Gracious! Missional! Diverse! Spirit-filled! Deep! Many terms come to mind when describing churches. How would you describe a healthy church?

Unfortunately churches are often defined by "nickels and noses" - the size of the budget and the numbers in the pews. Both measures are inadequate. A church may be very large and growing expansively because of its charismatic preacher, its professional praise band, its large staff and diverse programs. A church down the street may be very small because it ministers primarily to the social outcast, the poor, the marginalized. Neither is "better" than the other.

Let's look at four areas: Doctrine, Worship, Church Life, and Leadership.

> *"The local church is—or ought to be—a family, a local expression of the worldwide family of God, whose members regard, love, and treat one another as brothers and sisters."* [16]
> -John R.W. Stott

Doctrine

- Is there a clear Statement of Faith?
- Is it true and orthodox in its essential doctrines of God, Jesus, the Holy Spirit, the Trinity, the true church, and the Word of God, as defined by the historic creeds of the Christian faith?
- Is it in accordance with your conviction on other non-essential but important church practices and policies?
- Is there balance between worship, nurture and evangelism in the church?

Worship

Some years ago a writer in *Leadership Journal* suggested that people learn in primarily three different ways: *auditory, visual, and emotional.* These natural "bents" are also reflected in the way in which they are moved to worship God. Some people are primarily auditory: what they hear preached and taught is of greatest importance. Some people are more visual: the atmosphere and the images inspire respect and reverence for God. God's careful design for the temple of Jerusalem reveals His concern for the visual aspects of worship. Some people are more emotional, and what they sense and feel in worship is what matters most. You cannot read the Psalms without sensing the depth of feeling in David's prayers, praises and petitions to the God he loved.

> "What grips my heart every day is the knowledge that the radical message of [Jesus Christ's] transforming love has been given to the church." [17]
> -Bill Hybels

None of these three has greater value than the other; it is just the way people are "wired." Some denominations are characterized by one or the other of these particular strengths, while some wisely seek to include all in order to effectively lead everyone into a spirit of worship, which is a primary function of the church. Here are some ways of thinking of these three areas and relating them to the worship in a particular congregation:

Auditory

- Is the Word of God central in the worship? Is it read, quoted, explained, declared? Are passages preached fully, or does the speaker jump from one passage to another?

- Is the largest amount of worship time given to the preaching of the Word?
- Are the worshipers given tools or keywords to remember— to carry the message home?
- Is the preaching understandable to lay people? Does it avoid dense and difficult terminology? Is the truth applied, so that it is actionable on Monday morning?
- Is prayer a large part of the worship? Do lay people participate and do they sound familiar with God?
- Is the music joyful, thoughtful, Scriptural? Do the lyrics reflect the timeless truth of the Word, whether the style is classical or contemporary?
- Is the service performance-oriented, by a select few, or are lay people involved?

Visual:

- Is the church kept clean, orderly and consistent with reverence for a holy God? There may be pictures, banners, stained-glass windows or none of those, but the worshipers can sense that this is a place set apart to honor God and to revere His name.
- It may be formal or humble, a cathedral or a store front, but is it clearly designed to focus on the vertical relationship of man to his God?

Emotional:

- Do the faces of the congregation reflect genuine joy at being in God's house? Do they sing with enthusiasm, carry their Bibles, greet visitors warmly?
- Do you sense reverence for God, the "audience of one" in worship?
- Are there signs of disunity, anger, dissention?
- Does the preaching reach the "heart" as well as the "head?"
- Are children welcomed and celebrated?
- Are the sacraments inclusive, but clearly for believers?

> "The Lutheran Confessions stipulate that the church is simply marked by God's Word, in oral and sacramental forms. The church exists where the Gospel is rightly proclaimed and the sacraments are rightly administered, or the church is holy believers, lambs who are listening to the voice of the Shepherd." [18]
>
> - Robert Kolb

Church Life

- Are there programs for teaching children, youth, men and women?
- Are there opportunities for corporate as well as intercessory prayer?
- Do people appear to enjoy being together? Are there small groups for more intimate body-life, if the congregation is large enough? Is there laughter in the foyer?
- Does the budget reflect a spirit of generosity, of outreach, of ministry beyond mere self-preservation?
- Is there a diversity of the membership in cultural, economic, or racial backgrounds that reflects the community as a whole?

Leadership

- Is the pastor well-trained? Is he a shepherd, a true servant-leader? Is he available to people, or does he isolate himself in his office? Are his love for God and for people evident?
- Are lay people involved at all levels of church leadership? Are they accountable to the members?
- Is the church engaged in the community, rather than insulated or isolated?
- Are people encouraged to discover and use their spiritual gifts? Are new believers becoming active and involved?

On balance:

"A church that emphasizes only worship will end up with inadequate Bible teaching of believers and its members will remain shallow in their understanding of Scripture and immature in their Christian lives. If it also begins to neglect evangelism the church will cease to grow and influence others; it will become ingrown and eventually begin to wither.

A church that places the edification of believers as a purpose that takes precedence over the other two will tend to produce Christians who know much Bible doctrine but have spiritual dryness in their lives because they know little of the joy of worshiping God or telling others about Christ.

But a church that makes evangelism such a priority that it causes the other two purposes to be neglected will also end up with immature Christians who emphasize growth in numbers but have less and less genuine love for God expressed in their worship and less and less doctrinal maturity and personal holiness in their lives. All three purposes must be emphasized in a healthy church.

What about ministries of mercy and justice?

Accompanying the work of evangelism is also a ministry of mercy, a ministry that includes caring for the poor and needy in the name of the Lord...but such ministries should never become a substitute for genuine evangelism or for the other areas of ministry to God and to believers.*"* [19]

-Dr. Wayne Grudem

Beware: Some signs of an unhealthy church:

Top-heavy programming: too many programs being staffed by too few. This usually results in a very exhausted group of volunteers, often laboring outside of their spiritual giftedness. Visitors can be seen less as members of the family than as new workers to share the load.

Pastoral dictatorship: a leader who views the church as his own kingdom to be manipulated and used as he wishes, rather than under the authority of the congregation. Many churches have grown quickly under the inspiring and charismatic skills of such a leader, but they may just as quickly collapse when he falters or leaves.

A business-model of organization: From a *Christianity Today* editorial titled, *Sub-biblical Transformation:* "Biblical transformation of the church focuses not on social dynamics of corporate life—on mission statements, adaptive change, or mobilizing members. Such organizational principles can help any social organism, Christian or not. But to focus on them is to major in minors. In our managerial age, we instinctively look to 'leadership principles' and 'keys to effectiveness' to 'master dysfunctional congregations; organization-speak has a way of deafening our ears to the unique language of Scripture. Only that language can open our eyes to see 'the glory of the Lord,' the one reality that transforms us into Christ's image 'from one degree of glory to another.'...the world is not longing to see more people conformed to the image of organizational man, but to see people transformed into the image of "'he man Christ Jesus.*' "* (I Timothy. 2:5) [20]

Other: un-addressed sin such as gossip, adultery, slander, or dishonesty within the church; lethargy and entrenched, stagnant leadership; over-emphasis on single issues that define a congregation, such as political or social causes or alliances.

For further reading on the healthy church:

"*Eight Qualities of Healthy Churches*", Christian A. Schwarz in *Natural Church Development*, quoted in *Leadership Journal*, summer, 1997. "*20 Questions to Determine Your Church's Health*", Donald Bubna in the same LJ issue; "*Denominational Diagnostics*", Philip Yancey in *Christianity Today*, Nov. 2008; "*Your Church's Apgar*", Kevin A. Miller at www.Christianitytoday.com; *Becoming Your Favorite Church*, H.B. London, Jr. and Neil B. Wiseman (see bibliography); Mark Dever's *Nine Marks of a Healthy Church*, at www.ninemarks.com.; Ken Sande, *Transforming Your Church* (booklet from Peacemaker Ministries www.HisPeace.org)

The Mission of the Church

It all began with a girlfriend—a girlfriend who knew Jesus. Ceil Starr, an Orthodox Jewish girl, had recently married Moishe, and together they decided they would be "modern American Jews", not particularly religious, but valuing their heritage. But then Ceil became a believer in Christ the Messiah after her friend shared her faith. Ceil told her young husband who, in anger and determination to prove her wrong, began to study the Bible. There he, too, met Christ. From that conversion in the mid 1950's, grew the worldwide ministry known as "Jews for Jesus," through which thousands upon thousands of God's chosen people came to believe in Jesus, their Messiah. Moishe Rosen, according to historian Ruth A. Tucker, "was the most colorful Jewish evangelist of the 20th century—perhaps since the apostle Paul."

It all began with a personal testimony.

- Story told by Ruth Tucker [21]

It is Written...

"Jesus came to (the disciples) and said, 'All authority in heaven and on earth has been given to me. Therefore go and make disciples of all nations, baptizing them in the name of the Father and of the Son and of the Holy Spirit, and teaching them to obey everything I have commanded you. And surely I will be with you always, to the very end of the age.'" (Matthew 28:18-20)

Jesus to his disciples just before His ascension back to heaven. "You will receive power when the Holy Spirit comes on you; and you will be my witnesses in Jerusalem, and in all Judea and Samaria, and to the ends of the earth." (Acts 1:8)

The mission of the church can be summarized as ***evangelism***—both local and worldwide—and ***teaching.*** The goal is that lost people everywhere hear and believe the Good News of salvation through Christ Jesus, and that they grow in faith and knowledge of Him. Tim Dearborn explains in his book, *Beyond Duty: A Passion for Christ, a Heart for Mission*: "Christian mission is not our arrogant pursuit of other people to make them like us. Rather, it is our participation in God's pursuit of all people to make them like Him, and their lives like His."[22] Missions may involve compassionate ministry to the medical, educational and social needs of lost people, but the Cross must be central. The primary message is the Gospel—the Good News that Christ has come to reconcile lost mankind to God. Good works are the fruit of that Good News.

Evangelism is just one beggar telling another where to find bread.

- D.T. Niles [23]

Evangelism

The mission of the newly-born church after Pentecost began with the great mission work of the apostles which is told in the book of Acts. Paul, on his three missionary journeys, planted churches throughout the known world, and paid for his service with his life—as countless others have since. The church grew under great persecution and finally under the approval and sanction of various governments. As the church grew, so also did successive waves of corruption and renewal, but always there were efforts to spread the Gospel of Jesus Christ to the world. Some of the earliest missionaries are seldom mentioned any more, but their work should be remembered. Among them were:

- **Patrick**, who evangelized Ireland in the 400's. Over thirty years of ministry most of the country had been converted to Christ.
- **Boniface**, an English missionary known as the "Apostle to the Germans" who evangelized that country in the 700's.
- **Anskar,** known as the "Apostle of the North" who spread the Gospel to Sweden in the 800's.
- Missionary brothers from Greece, **Cyril and Methodius**, who translated the Scriptures into Slavonic, and saw multitudes come to faith, also in the 800's.
- **Francis Xavier**, founder of the Jesuits, who ministered in India and Japan and is thought to have brought between 100,000—300,000 converts to Christianity in the 1500's.
- **Mattoo Ricci**, who evangelized China in the 1600's. The Kublai Khan had requested through Marco Polo that one hundred Christian scholars be sent to his country centuries before, but only three had come, and that opportunity for evangelism had been lost. [24]

The more modern era of missions was rooted in three great renewal movements: **Pietism, Methodism and the Great Awakening**, which led to the "Great Century of Missions"—the 19th century. Philip Jakob Spener (1635-1705), sometimes called "The Second Luther" began a renewal movement in Europe that emphasized the power of the Word of God, personal conversion, holy living, fellowship and witness to a lost world. Out of this movement missionaries went to many lands concentrating on evangelism, Bible translation, training indigenous leadership, and education. The 1700's also saw the conversion of John and Charles Wesley, the founders of Methodism (so-called because of their emphasis on certain spiritual disciplines). The church spread rapidly in England and throughout the West. The Great Awakening in New England, led by Jonathan Edwards and George Whitefield saw revival spread throughout the nation and ignite passion for world evangelism. A Second Great Awakening from the late 1700's to 1820 once again spread revival through North America.

Some prominent missionaries from the "**Great Century of World Missions" (**the 19th century) **include:**

William Carey, often called "the father of modern missions," who spent a lifetime ministering in India. Together with two other friends, all based at a station called Serampore, they preached the Word and translated the Scriptures. His personal life was tragic, as his wife and children all died of the diseases common in India. Much of his translation work was also destroyed by fire—but Christ was victorious and the Gospel spread rapidly. (Incidentally, Danish Lutheran missionaries were in the area presently called Indonesia one hundred years before Carey.)

Robert Morrison, followed by **James Hudson Taylor**, in China. At great personal cost, Taylor founded the China Inland Mission. He was known for crossing cultural barriers, dressing in Chinese clothing and identifying with the people he came to evangelize.

Adoniram and Ann Judson, who pioneered missionary work in Burma (Myanmar). Ann literally kept her husband alive while he was captive during a period of war.

David Livingstone and his father-in-law, **Robert Moffat,** evangelized many areas of Africa and inspired countless others to foreign missionary work.

Yi Sung-Hun, an influential scholar who is considered to have been the first Korean Christian and who led thousands to Christ. He was later martyred for his faith.

Count Nicolaus von Zinzendorf, whose efforts brought Christ to Greenland and elsewhere through the work of the Moravians.

Pandita Ramabai, a respected and educated woman who gave her life to serving and educating the poor in India.

David Brainerd, a young, passionate missionary to American Indians.

Later came the great revivalist preachers, such as D.L. Moody, Billy Sunday, and Billy Graham, under whose preaching thousands came to faith. In the later 20th century and continuing today, great numbers of people, particularly in Africa and South America are being converted under the Pentecostal/charismatic movement. Even under terrible persecution and abuse Christianity is spreading in countries which are closed to the "official" preaching of the Gospel. The technology of radio, television, and the internet have greatly expanded the reach of the Gospel throughout the world. The Holy Spirit is at work, calling lost people to be reconciled to God through faith in Jesus Christ.

Teaching—Education

> It is Written...
>
> Philip was told by the Spirit of God to approach a chariot where an important Ethiopian official was reading the prophet Isaiah. "Do you understand what you are reading?" Philip asked. 'How can I,' he said, 'unless someone explains it to me?' So he invited Philip to come up and sit with him...The eunuch asked Philip, 'Tell me, please, who is the prophet talking about, himself or someone else?'" Then Philip began with that very passage of Scripture and told him the good news about Jesus." (Acts 8:30-35)

The second mission of the church is ***education***, bringing the knowledge of Christ and His Word to believers, leading them to mature faith and service.

In the local congregation this usually involves all ages: Sunday School for all ages, catechism for youth, and small-group Bible studies, (often separate for men and women) in addition to preaching. Christian Education Boards usually oversee this ministry. Volumes and volumes of resources on education in the church have been written, and graduate degrees may be obtained at many seminaries and Bible schools, so summarizing the topic is impossible. It is enough to recognize the necessity of teaching and to carefully plan the manner in which it is done in a local church. Some objectives to be considered in a Lutheran church include:

> "It is not so much the case that God has a mission for the church in the world, as that God has a church for his mission in the world. Our mission flows from God's mission. Christian mission means the committed and obedient participation of the church in the mission of God to bring about the blessing of the nations and redemption of creation....God's mission requires all God's people and all God's gifting and calling, distributed among his people for every kind of service, in the church and in the world."[25]
>
> -Alister McGrath

1. Leading children and adults to personal faith, growth and maturity in Christ.
2. Familiarizing students with Bible structure and basic teachings.
3. Acquainting students with the historical sequence of the Bible rather than with scattered people and events.
4. Beginning and encouraging life-long Bible study and memorization. Though they may not fully understand the meaning, children are able to store the Word in their hearts, and the Spirit will use it throughout their lives to instruct and encourage them.
5. Helping young people understand that they may move from their baptism to a mature and personal faith in Christ without having to take the trip of a prodigal "into a far country."
6. Teaching and modeling Christian living and a personal walk with God.
7. Familiarizing students with distinctive teachings and history of the Lutheran Church.
8. Building friendship and fellowship between believers.
9. Providing an opportunity for Christian service by teachers and staff.

The importance of this teaching is clearly demonstrated in the research of Christian Smith, from the National Study of Youth and Religion at the University of North Carolina at Chapel Hill. He found some ideas among young people that caused great concern and that inspire us to teach them more effectively.

Their religion could be summed up by three words: **Moralistic Therapeutic Deism**. That is, there is a God who created and watches over the world, He wants us to be fair and good, but the only time it really matters is when you're in trouble. Most of the three thousand teens who were interviewed had little idea of the basics of their faith, and viewed God more as a familiar friend, and less as God Almighty. The startling fact was that many of these respondents identified themselves as Christians who had grown up in church.

It is clear that education in the church must be much more carefully planned and teachers called who will model an authentic life of faith and obedience to the inerrant Word of God.

Luther's Small Catechism, which is used to instruct young people in the Lutheran Church, is a compilation of questions and answers that cover the essential doctrines of the church. Martin Luther first compiled his catechism in 1529. The *Explanation of the Catechism* used by my Lutheran denomination is based on the one written by the Danish Lutheran pastor, Dr. Erik Pontoppidan in 1737. Topics include the *10 Commandments, the three Articles of the Creed, the seven petitions of the Lord's Prayer, and the Sacraments of Baptism and the Lord's Supper.* This edition includes 387 questions and answers. The instruction, which is usually given over two or three years to middle-school young people, concludes with a Confirmation service. In most Lutheran churches this has historically included a vow or a commitment to believe in and follow Christ. Other Lutheran churches, fearing that such a confession made under social pressure could lead to hypocrisy, view Confirmation rather as a ceremony honoring those who complete the instruction. Students are often asked to write or speak a personal testimony of faith, but generally are not required to do so.

> Dennis E. Williams, writes in *The Portable Seminary*:
>
> "The purpose of Christian education is to bring people to a saving faith in Jesus Christ, to train them in a life of discipleship, and to equip them for service in the world today. It is to develop in believers a biblical worldview that will assist them in making significant decisions from a Christian perspective. It is helping believers to "think Christianly" about all areas of life so that they can impact society with the message of the gospel. In essence, it is the development of a Christian worldview." [26]

In the Appendix of this book are listed publishers of Sunday School and other Christian Education curriculum materials. Many are identified by denominational affiliation so that their particular doctrinal distinctives may be recognized. There are primarily two Lutheran publishers of Christian education materials: Augsburg-Fortress, and Concordia. However, many Lutheran congregations use materials from a wide variety of other non-denominational publishers. It is always wise to read the Statement of Faith of such materials (often found on their websites) in order to be certain of the truth on essential doctrines.

For further reading about the mission of the church: An excellent summary of mission history is in *The Portable Seminary,* David Horton, editor; excellent biographies of missionaries and mission movements are in *Christian History* magazine; the U.S. Center for World Mission publishes "Mission Frontiers" magazine and website which include much current information, and your church library or your pastor's library will undoubtedly include many books on both missions and Christian Education.

Trends in the 21st Century Church

- **"Seeker-sensitive" churches**

These churches, often led by highly gifted, charismatic pastors, have had great influence among the Protestant churches in the latter half of the last century and into the present. Among the best-known are Saddleback Church in California, led by Pastor Rick Warren, and Willowbrook Church in suburban Chicago, let by Pastor Bill Hybels. These churches, and others like them, are usually evangelical in doctrinal views, their leaders have become well-known through their books and influence among other church leaders, and they may be of various denominational affiliations, but most would describe themselves as non-denominational. Their focus is on bringing the Gospel to secular people by being open and approachable, by avoiding "theology-speak", by preaching to the perceived needs of people, and by attracting congregants through excellence and diversity in programming and worship styles. They are sometimes accused of being entertainment-centered, and because many are huge there may be less commitment, loyalty, and fellowship than in a smaller congregation. But their passion is to reach people with the Gospel. As with any movement, there have been abuses and issues with accountability, but God has been at work and many people have come to true faith in Jesus Christ.

- **House churches**

At the opposite extreme of the mega-churches are the growing number of house churches. Here groups of families and friends meet for worship, Bible study and prayer in an attempt to model the early church of Acts. They value relationships, fellowship, commitment, simplicity and accountability, in reaction to the anonymity of huge congregations.

- **The "Emergent" church**

Seen as a reaction to traditional evangelical churches, the emergent church movement is growing, adapting and evolving. Its main purpose is to use any and all means in order to reach postmoderns with the Gospel of Jesus Christ. Within the movement there is great diversity and a range of doctrinal positions, from relatively conservative to quite radical and sometimes truly heretical, particularly when denying the authority and inerrancy of the Word.

> "While the traditional evangelical view begins with facts, which influence belief, which influence behavior, the emerging church begins with experience, which influences behavior, which influences belief."[27]
>
> -Dan Kimball

To understand this movement one must understand both *worldview* and the *postmodern worldview.*

Worldview simply refers to the set of beliefs that all people have which shape their attitudes towards all of life, particularly the big questions of: Who am I? Where did I come from? What is the meaning of life, if there is a meaning? Is there a God? If so, is He knowable? What happens when we die? People may not verbalize these beliefs but still their actions are influenced by them. For example, if there is no God to whom men are ultimately accountable there is little reason to be concerned about behavior that may offend such a God. If there is no meaning in life—no purpose for existence—then people may search for some meaning in any way that brings them pleasure regardless of its affect on others.

The ***Postmodern worldview*** is explained more fully in the section, "*Because you asked...*" in Chapter 3, but David Horton offers this definition in *The Portable Seminary:* [Postmodernism is] "a worldview that is skeptical of absolute truths or universal principles in favor of relativity and individual experience. In this view, no single answer or paradigm suffices for all cultures or individuals; reality is subject to individual interpretation.*"*[28] The phrase that is sometimes heard, "That may be true for you but it is not true for me," is a clear expression of the Postmodern worldview.

Some of the best-known leaders in the movement at present are Brian McLaren of Emergent Village, Dan Kimball, Mark Driscoll, Rob Bell, Doug Pagitt, and Tony Jones. Scott McKnight, professor of religious studies at North Park Theological Seminary in Chicago, expresses his views in identifying **five "streams" of the Emerging church** in an extensive 2007 article in *Christianity Today*:[29]

1. **Prophetic.** (or at least Provocative). They admit that they sometimes exaggerate and provoke in an attempt to produce change. Some can sound irreverent and mean-spirited.
2. **Postmodern**. Most in the movement see themselves as either intentionally ministering ***to*** or ***with*** postmodern people. They associate with and accept postmodernity as a fact of life in the world, a condition in which the Gospel is to be proclaimed. Most do not see themselves ***as*** postmoderns—but some on the more radical edges do.
3. **Praxis-Oriented** (praxis just means "how the faith is lived out.") They acknowledge that beliefs are essential, but are equally as concerned about the fruit of that belief being evident in changed lives. They may be more experience-oriented and creative in their worship than traditional churches. They are intentionally missional—seeking to engage the community, to reach out beyond the walls of the sanctuary to needy people, caring not only about lost souls but also about hurting bodies, struggling families, and unjust societies.
4. **Post-Evangelical**. Within the movement there is a rejection of the rigid doctrine and systematic theology that they see among evangelicals. They are more accepting of diverse views and more humble about their own convictions. Of course, taken to the extreme, this can lead them to tolerance of false teaching. McKnight warns his emergent friends to be careful that the goal is always to point to salvation through Jesus Christ. Though he would describe himself as emergent, he warns, "This emerging ambivalence about who is in and who is out creates a serious problem for evangelism. The emerging movement is not known for it, but I wish it were. Unless you proclaim the Good News of Jesus Christ, there is no good news at all—and if there is no Good News, then there is no Christianity, emerging or evangelical."[30]
5. **Political.** People within the emergent movement tend to be more left-leaning politically than most evangelicals. Because of their concern for social justice issues they may support liberal politicians, despite their disagreement on moral issues such as abortion and the sanctity of marriage. They are usually highly critical of the actions of the Religious Right.

Viewed most positively, the Emergent Church movement is a courageous attempt to reach out missionally, to break out of traditional patterns which they see as dated and ineffective, and to passionately follow Christ's example of concern for social justice for the poor and disenfranchised. Viewed more critically, there is concern that some of the more radical leaders have embraced relativism, are vague on essential doctrines of the church, and weak on the authority and inerrancy of Scripture. Many use some provocative means in order to connect with their young audiences—means that are viewed as offensive to many. Christians must be especially discerning of false teaching that may not be Christian at all, though claiming to be so. (See Chapter 3: *Twisted Truth: Heresies and False Teaching.*)

A sampling of the range of teaching by leaders within the movement is *An Emergent Manifesto of Hope* by Doug Pagitt and Tony Jones. [31]

- **Revival of interest in Ancient Worship**

Among the younger generation of postmodern people there appears to be a hunger for deep religious or spiritual experience. With that has come a resurgence of interest in ancient worship styles of music and liturgy and sometimes of the atmosphere and architecture that accompany such worship. The informality so valued by the earlier generation of baby boomers is now seen by many as less reverent and meaningful in approaching the presence of God. Interest in the spiritual disciplines of meditation and fasting is also being revived. This trend has been noted in the secular press as well as influential evangelical sources such as *Christianity Today*. (see February, 2008, page 22 on ancient worship; March, 2006, page 112 on meditation and retreat; May, 2008, page 39 on the return to liturgical practices, and May, 2009, on architecture.)

- **Decline of denominations**

Several factors have lead to the steady decline of many denominations, at least within the United States:

1. The rise and success of large, non-denominational churches. Though many of them may have informal denominational ties, and their pastors have distinct doctrinal views, they do not identify themselves as such. Sometimes the reason is to break down perceived barriers in order to reach a broad range of people. Or sometimes it may reflect an openness towards diverse doctrinal positions, at least in non-essentials.
2. The growth in attendance and vitality among evangelical churches as opposed to mainline denominations. This steady decline has been noted for decades.
3. The turbulence among denominations over issues of inerrancy of the Word and social issues such as gay marriage and the ordination of homosexual clergy. A number of mainline denominations have splintered as a result, and individual congregations may become independent rather than continue to affiliate contrary to their convictions. A disillusionment with hierarchal authority has often accompanied this trend.
4. Some very large congregations do not see the need for the services provided by denominational leadership any longer. They are large enough to sponsor their own mission programs, publish their own materials, plant new churches, and train their own leadership.

- **Missional Theology**

Missional theology emphasizes the need for churches to break out of their isolation and traditions in order to go to seek the lost rather than wait for the lost to come to them. Many strategies are being employed in an effort to more effectively carry out the Great Commission, though some concerns remain about excesses and compromises. A most critical area of concern is the view of the Word as the highest authority in all matters of faith and life. Anything less compromises truth for the sake of unity. Missional theology can also easily morph into social action as a substitute for evangelism.

The Church of the Lutheran Brethren has just completed an extensive statement on the issue which is available through their administrative offices.

- **Evangelical Feminism**

  The subject of the leadership of women in the church—and specifically the ordination of women— is the center of much current debate and division. The two primary views are ***egalitarian*** (that all roles in ministry are available to people regardless of gender), and ***complementarian*** (that women and men are equally created by God and gifted for leadership and service, but that some specific roles—such as pastor and elder— are carefully designated by God as the responsibility of men. There is no suggestion of inferiority, but rather of responsibility.)

  The two views of the leadership of women in the church are well-explored in John Piper and Wayne Grudem's *Recovering Biblical Manhood and Womanhood*: *A Response to Evangelical Feminism*; Wayne Grudem's *Evangelical Feminism and Biblical Truth: An Analysis of More Than 100 Disputed Questions*; and Sarah Sumner's *Men and Women in the Church.* (See Bibliography)

- **Other issues**—such as the Open Theology debate regarding God's sovereign will and whether He knows the future fully, the Atonement debate represented primarily by N.T. Wright and John Piper, the tension between Pietism and Confessional Lutheranism, the rise of the Religious Left with their emphasis on social justice, and dialogue between evangelicals and Roman Catholics to seek common ground and to join in the shared passion to protect the life of the unborn— are huge and important topics that cannot be covered in these pages, but which deserve the attention of thoughtful Christians. Consult your pastor for relevant resources for study, or follow the discussions in current Christian journals and online resources such as The Gospel Coalition Blog (web@thegospelcoalition.org) and others. Most importantly, study the Bible directly for yourself, praying for guidance from the Holy Spirit.

Endnotes:

---

1. Richard K. Avery and Donald S. March, "I Am the Church", in *Sing to the Lord* (Ventura, CA: Gospel Light, 1976).
2. C. S. Lewis, quoted in Alister E. McGrath, gen. ed., *Zondervan Handbook of Christian Beliefs* (Grand Rapids: Zondervan, 2005), 215.
3. Rev. Joseph H. Levang, *Living Lutheran Christianity: A Historical Sketch of Lutheran Pietism* (Fergus Falls, MN: Faith & Fellowship Publishing, 1991), 82-120.
4. "*We Believe...Statement of Faith*" (Fergus Falls, MN: Faith & Fellowship Publishing, rev. 2007). Pamphlet, available at www.faithandfellowship.org.
5. John R. W. Stott, "Evangelism Plus", an interview with Tim Stafford, *Christianity Today*, (October, 2006), 94.
6. Wayne Grudem, *Systematic Theology, An Introduction to Biblical Doctrine* (Grand Rapids: Zondervan, 1994), 867-868.

7. Erik Pontoppidan. Warren Olsen and David Rinden, eds. *Explanation of Luther's Small Catechism,* 2nd Edition (Fergus Falls, MN: Faith & Fellowship Publishing, 1988), 53
8. Ibid., 60.
9. Ibid., 75
10. F. L. Cross and E. A. Livingstone, eds. *Dictionary of the Christian Church* (Peabody, MA: Hendrickson Publishers, Inc., 2007), 1772. (Published by arrangement with Oxford University Press).
11. Ibid., 1229, 1253, 1773, 1573, 462, 1351.
12. Tim Ysteboe, *We Believe: A Commentary on the Statement of Faith* (Fergus Falls, MN: Faith and Fellowship Publishing, 2009), 149.
13. Ibid., 149.
14. Grudem, *Systematic Theology*, 936.
15. Ysteboe, *We Believe*, 150.
16. John R. W. Stott, *Life in Christ* (Grand Rapids: Baker, 2003), 82. Quoted in David Horton, gen. ed., *The Portable Seminary* (Bloomington, MN: Bethany House Publishers, 2006), 183.
17. Bill Hybels, *Courageous Leadership* (Grand Rapids: Zondervan, 2002), 21.
18. Robert Kolb, *The Christian Faith* (St. Louis: Concordia Publishing, 1993), 268. In reference to Smalcald Articles III:XII, 2, *The Book of Concord,* trans. and ed. Theodore G. Tappert (Philadelphia: Fortress, 1959), 315.
19. Grudem, *Systematic Theology*, 868-869.
20. "Sub-biblical Transformation", editorial in *Christianity Today* (June, 2007), 27.
21. Ruth Tucker, "An Evangelist With Chutzpah", *Christianity Today* (July, 2010), 39.
22. Tim Dearborn, *Beyond Duty: A Passion for Christ, A Heart for Mission* (Monrovia, CA: World Vision Resources, 1997)
23. D. T. Niles, quoted in Alister E. McGrath, *Zondervan Handbook of Christian Beliefs* (Grand Rapids: Zondervan, 2005), 236.
24. "Christian History Timeline", (Torrance, CA: Rose Publishing, Inc., 1998, 2009). Pamphlet.
25. McGrath, 258.
26. Dennis E. Williams, "Defining Christian Education", David Horton, gen. ed. *The Portable Seminary* (Bloomington, MN: Bethany House Publishers, 2006), 642.
27. Dan Kimball, *The Emerging Church* (Grand Rapids: Zondervan, 2004), 187.
28. Horton, *The Portable Seminary,* 695.
29. Scott McKnight, "Five Streams of the Emerging Church", *Christianity Today*, (February, 2007), 35.
30. Ibid., 38.
31. Doug Pagitt and Tony Jones, *An Emergent Manifesto of Hope* (Grand Rapids, MI: Baker Books, 2007).

Chapter 3

Twisted Truth: Heresies and False Teaching

Twisted Truth: Heresies and False Teaching

Heresy: The word means "choice" and refers to teachings that contradict accepted orthodox views.
Orthodox: The term was coined by church father, Irenaeus, to characterize what most Church Fathers agreed was the truth.

"The greatest challenge for serious Christians today is not re-inventing Christianity, but redis-covering its core teach-ings."[1]
-Charles Colson

Why does it matter that I recognize historical heresies?

- **Truth:** The inerrancy of the Bible is at the core of what we believe, and any teaching that discredits or denies or distorts the truth of the Word is dangerous.
- **Repetition**: The same old heresies occur over and over throughout church history. They may appear with a new face, but they are the same old issues.
- **Diversion**: Arguing over and again about what is settled doctrinal truth only distracts the church from its mission to evangelize the world.
- **Destruction:** The enemy of our souls and of the church seeks to destroy God and His people. The ugliness of his face behind much controversy is rarely seen, but he is at work to ruin souls whom Christ died to redeem.

"The greatest challenge of evan-gelicalism is to re-catechize our churches."[2]
-J.I. Packer

"It is obvious to me that doctrine matters. Some years ago, I visited Sri Lanka, just after Anglican Bishop David Jenkins was reported to have dismissed the Resurrection as a "conjuring trick with bones." (It was later revealed that he had been misquoted.) Our ministry leader, who escorted me through the country's prisons, told me the news had cost many conversions, because Buddhists and Hindus used it to convince people that Christianity is based on a mere trick.

Clearly, when we stop taking seriously the historical truths of the church, we undermine our witness, often with far-reaching consequences. For example, Muslim student groups today proselytize with pamphlets asserting that Christians worship three Gods: Father, Mother, and Son. Where did they get that idea? From seventh-century Egyptian Christians who gave up on the Bible and embraced this heresy.

Last June, a Pew Forum on Religion and Public Life survey found rampant doctrinal ignorance among American Christians. Fifty-seven percent of evangelicals believed people who follow religions other than their own can enjoy eternal life. The results were so unexpected that Pew repeated the survey, asking more specific questions. The answers were virtually unchanged. Astonishingly, about half believed that everyone, atheists included, was going to end up in heaven. Heaven for the godless? That's the old heresy of universalism... Some embrace another old heresy, that doctrines must be extracted from inward experience—that is, personal feelings. That's a version of Gnosticism."[3]

-Charles Colson

Heresies in Church History

Most heresies involve two primary teachings of Scripture: The Trinity (Father, Son and Holy Spirit) and the Incarnation of Christ (His deity and His humanity).

Heresy:	Date:	Meaning:
Gnosticism	Began in the early church, but reappears through the centuries	From Greek word, "gnosis, meaning "knowledge." Emphasizes secret knowledge and secret rituals. Salvation consists of experiencing these. Includes pantheism (that God and creation are one); the material world is evil and an illusion, man has a "divine inner being"; Jesus is not really human, he just appeared to be.
Docetism	1st century	Believed the deity of Jesus, but denied His humanity. Jesus only "appeared" to be human.
Ebiontism	1st century	Denied the virgin birth and deity of Christ. Jesus was only a human prophet. Taught that Christians should submit to OT law, and rejected the teachings of Paul.
Adoptionism	2nd century	Taught that Jesus was born as only human, but became divine when God "adopted" Him.
Manicheanism	2nd century	Combined Christianity with Zoroastrian and Buddhist beliefs; popular until the 600's, and included Augustine before his conversion to Christ.
Marcionism	2nd century	Tried to corrupt the canon by rejecting the OT and some NT books. Taught that the NT God of love and grace was inconsistent with the "vengeful" God of the OT.
Modalism (also called *Sabellianism*)	2nd century	Denied the Trinity. There is only one God who showed Himself in three modes or forms. Praxeas, likely the founder of the heresy, said the Father became His own Son.
Montanism	2-3rd centuries	Taught the end of the world was near; Holy Spirit was giving him new revelations. Montanus led his followers in strict, ascetic lifestyle with emphasis on manifestations of gifts of the Holy Spirit. Identified their three leaders with God the Father, Son, Holy Spirit. Condemned by Council of Constantinople in AD 382.

Heresy (continued)	Date:	Meaning:
Apollinarianism	4th century	Denied true humanity of Christ; He had a human body and soul but not a human spirit or human reason.
Arianism	4th century	Denied that Christ was eternal; said Christ was created by God. Condemned by Council of Nicea 325 AD. The Nicene, Chalcedonian and Athanasian Creeds were in response to this heresy.
Macedonianism	4th century	Similar to Arianism in denying Christ has the same essence with God, but said He was nevertheless eternal. Also denied the divinity of the Holy Spirit.
Pelagianism	4th century	Denied the total depravity (sinfulness) of man; man is not accountable for what he could not help; he is innocent and therefore able to initiate salvation by himself. Salvation means choosing to follow Jesus' example.
Nestorianism	5th century	Christ had two natures or persons—one divine and the other human; they were not united.
Eutychianism (also called the Monophysite heresy)	5th century	In reaction to Nestorians, taught that Christ had only one nature. The divine nature and the human nature had each been so modified to accommodate each other that He was neither genuinely divine nor human.

How do I recognize a "new" teaching as heresy?

You must study the Scriptures and compare what is being taught to the absolute truth of the Bible. Study the historic Creeds of the Christian Faith which summarize the essential truths that define genuine Christianity. (See Appendix 3 for four of the most familiar creeds). Visit with your pastor, who can clear up confusion and point you to the Scriptures.

Ask yourself:

- *Who do they say that God is*? Is He eternal, Almighty, the Creator?
- *Who do they say that Jesus Christ is?* Is He virgin-born? Fully human and fully divine? Did He exist from all eternity and is one with God the Father and God the Spirit? Did He rise from the dead?
- *Who is the Holy Spirit*? Is He truly God? Is He active today in believers and in the world?
- *What is the nature of man*? Is he truly fallen, and in need of salvation?
- *How can man be saved*? Can he initiate salvation by himself, by his own efforts? Is salvation only by grace through faith in Jesus Christ? Is he lost if he does not repent and is not converted?
- *Do they believe the Bible is totally and absolutely true, or does it just "contain" God's truth?* Was it true only for the culture in which it was written? Do they have new revelation about God?

Watch Out! False Teaching Today

Believers in Christ are warned throughout the Scriptures to be vigilant in their faith: to be knowledgeable about the godlessness in the culture, the cults or untrue religious systems, as well as the false teachings that can invade the church, masquerading as Biblical truth. In this age of tolerance and relativism, even committed Christians can become deceived. In fact, the Bible warns that there will be believers who will fall away from the faith.

A complete coverage of non-Christian religions, cults and false teachings cannot be given here, but many useful resources are listed for your further study. However, a list of non-Christian religious options, a list and brief explanation of prominent non-Christian religions, a list of most familiar cults, and a discussion of current false teaching fads is included.

Peter Kreeft and Ronald K. Tacelli, in *Handbook of Christian Apologetics* list **six fundamental non-Christian theological choices about God:**

1. **Agnosticism** ("I don't know") vs. belief ("I claim to know something")
2. **Atheism** (no gods) vs. theism (some kind of God or gods)
3. **Polytheism** (many gods) vs. monotheism (one God)
4. **Pantheism** (God = everything, and everything = God; God is immanent but not transcendent) vs. theism proper, or supernaturalism (a transcendent God)
5. **Deism** (God is real but remote; he has not revealed himself) vs. revealed theism (God is present and has made himself known);
6. **Unitarianism** (only one person in God), vs. trinitarianism (three persons in God) [4]

Non-Christian Religions and Cults [5]

Most will differ from historic Christianity in their view of the person of God, Jesus Christ, the Holy Spirit, the Trinity, how man can be saved, and life after death.

Eight Prominent Non-Christian Religions

Judaism (ancient Israel)
Hinduism (1800 B.C, India)
* *Hare Krishna* (1965, New York)
* *Transcendental Meditation* (1959, CA)
** *Buddism* (525 B.C., India)
Nichiren Shoshu Buddhism
(1253 A.D. Japan)
Islam (abt. 600 A.D., Saudi Arabia)
Baha'i World Faith (1844 A.D., Iran)

* Based on Hinduism
** Off-shoot of Hinduism

Prominent Cults

Armstrongism (Worldwide Ch. Of God)
Christian Science (Mary Baker Eddy, 1875)
Jehovah's Witnesses (Watchtower, 1879)
Mormonism—Latter-day Saints
(Joseph Smith, 1830)
New Age Spirituality
(based in Eastern mysticism, paganism)
Scientology (Ron Hubbard, 1954)
Spiritualism (Spiritism) 1848, NY
Unification Church
(Sun Myung Moon 1954, S. Korea)
Unity School of Christianity
(Charles and Myrtle Fillmore, 1889)

Characteristics of False Teachers

The apostle Peter writes in II Peter 2, "There were also false prophets among the people, just as there will be false teachers among you. They will secretly introduce destructive heresies, even denying the sovereign Lord who bought them—bringing swift destruction on themselves. Many will follow their shameful ways and will bring the way of truth into disrepute." Peter continues to describe them:

- They work from within the church, and are not outside ungodly influencers, so they are not as easy to detect.
- Their target is believers.
- They were once "on the path" (vs. 15): "They have left the straight way and wandered off to follow the way of Balaam son of Beor, who loved the wages of wickedness."
- Their methods include secretly introducing destructive heresies, appealing to vulnerable immature Christians, promising "freedom", denying the sovereign Lord, exploiting, slandering, blaspheming, seducing, appealing to lustful natures. They are secretive, crafty, influential, boastful, bold, and arrogant. But these characteristics may be masked.
- Their motives include greed. (vs. 3): "In their greed these teachers will exploit you with stories they have made up."
- The results? Believers are drawn away (vs. 2, 21), they bring shame upon the church (vs. 2), they are ultimately destroyed (vs. 3, 17).
- The promise for true and faithful believers? "The Lord knows how to rescue godly men from trials." (vs. 9).
- The clear warning is to WATCH OUT!

Contemporary False Teaching

"**God is Dead**" - a teaching with roots in the late 19th century and in the writings of Friedrich Nietzsche, but which again came into prominence in the 1970's in America. It is similar to deism, in that it acknowledges the existence of God, but teaches that He is impersonal, uninterested and uninvolved in the world today.

Liberation Theology—A school of thought that sees Jesus as liberator of the poor from social, economic and political oppression. It has most often been seen in Latin America and has sometimes been associated with Marxism and actual revolutionary activism.

Universalism—the belief that all people will ultimately be saved; none will go lost. "All roads lead to heaven."

"**Oneness Pentecostalism**", also known as "Jesus Only." It denies the Trinity, teaching that God has revealed Himself through His name, Jesus, and that there are only three "manifestations" of the one God. It is very similar to the old Modalism heresy.

Humanism—The belief that man is basically innately good from birth. The task of culture then is to teach, motivate and enhance the child—and sometimes just not interfere—so the child develops his full potential. It is characterized by a great hope in the goodness of man's nature. It has the effect of removing personal guilt: when behavior becomes destructive it can be blamed on exterior pressures and conditions rather than on personal fault. Obviously, then, there is no need for a Savior.

"Prosperity Gospel"

(also known as "name it/claim it", "word of faith", "health/wealth")

Popular teachers of the doctrine: Kenneth Copeland
Kenneth E. Hagin

Characteristics of the doctrine:

1. **"Positive confession"** - the ability to speak words to produce positive results in life. It assigns some special power to the speaking of words rather than just the believing of them.

2. **Believers have the right to wealth and health**. Hagin says, "We as Christians need not suffer financial setbacks; we need not be captive to poverty or sickness! God has provided healing and prosperity for His children...don't pray for money anymore. You have authority through my Name to claim prosperity." - Kenneth E. Hagin. [6]

3. Some teachers deny the **deity of Christ**. Kenneth Copeland writes, "You are all-God. You are to think the way Jesus thought. He didn't think it robbery to be equal with God." [7]

4. Some teachers deny the **inerrancy of Scripture.**

For further study on this doctrine and quotations from charismatic leaders who oppose it, and an extensive list of references, see *The Moody Handbook of Theology*, pages 678-682. (Bibliography).

"Pop Spirituality"

Currently fashionable views of "spirituality" (referring to the devotional practices of believers, similar to the earlier more familiar terms, "godliness" or "spiritual disciplines") which are taught by some of today's celebrities are dangerously close—if not nearly identical—to old heresies. Because they often include Scripture, they can easily deceive the unwary Christian. Some leading voices among them are Oprah Winfrey, Eckhart Tolle, Rhonda Byrne and Deepak Chopra.

Among some of the myths being taught are:

1. Every human is divine.
2. There are many paths to God.
3. The goal of my life is centered in me.
4. What I wish for determines what happens in my life.
5. God's Word is not the final authority.

For further study see *Pop Spirituality and the Truth: The Real Secret of a New Earth* by Timothy Paul Jones, (Torrance, CA: Rose Publishing, Inc., *2009).*

Because you asked....

What is meant by "worldview?"

The term "worldview" refers to a set of beliefs or perspectives which everyone has, which people hold about questions of life, such as, *Why am I? Where did I come from? Is there a God? What happens after death?* When we discuss "worldview" we consider how those beliefs affect our lives.

These beliefs may or may not be true, and may or may not be strongly or very consciously held, but they form the foundation upon which people make decisions and build their lives.

Christians, of course, begin and end with the truth of God as revealed in His Holy Word. It is their plumb-line against which every other teaching is measured. It is the absolute true revelation of God—who is the one true God—and His plan for mankind both universally and personally.

It is immensely important that the Christian worldview be well-taught to young people so they have a firm foundation and understanding of the Gospel before they are bombarded with the deluge of non-Christian worldviews as they attend college or in other ways begin to grow in awareness of other belief systems.

> *"You have made us for yourself and our heart is restless until it finds its rest in you."*
> Augustine of Hippo [8]

Alister McGrath on "worldview:"

"Everyone has a religion. Many people don't think that they do, of course. And that's because 'religion' for them means what we might call 'proper-noun' religion—Buddhism, Islam, Sikhism, and so on. But everyone has a central motivation in his or her life and everyone has a map of reality in his or her head, and the combination of motive and map we can call each person's functional religion. It's the defining centre of one's life, whether framed by traditions as old as Judaism or Hinduism, or by what one saw on the television last night or read on the Internet this morning....A coherent Christian world view—beyond whatever satisfaction and delight it may provide for the intellect—gives believers an interpretive frame within which they have the best opportunity to live as Christians in the most fundamental sense: to discern God's will and way, and thus to respond to Him best in faith—in humble, obedient, and grateful love." [9]

What is meant by Postmodernism?

Postmodernism is a worldview that has become dominant in western culture since perhaps 1980. It is talked about and written about everywhere, so is nearly impossible to summarize, but it is characterized by:

- **Relativism.** The idea that there is no such thing as objective truth or universal principles, regardless of culture or human reason. There is no truth that remains true no matter what my—or your—opinion is of it. You will hear, "*That may be true for you, but it is not true for me.*"
- **Tolerance** for all shades of experience and opinion. Few things are labeled truly "evil" or

"wrong" in all cases. The idea is commonly-expressed in the word, "Whatever!"

- **Reaction** to the apparent dominance and control of those individuals or governments who claim to have a corner on truth. Traditions are to be re-examined or discarded.
- **Rights**. Everyone should have the right—and should be encouraged—to believe as they please, by whatever route they choose, without any sense of evaluation or criticism.
- **Image**. This view values visual image over word, experience over doctrine, and story over lecture.
- **Relationships**. There is a strong emphasis on relationships.

How has this affected the church of Jesus Christ, whose truth claims are everywhere in Scripture, particularly as He claimed in John 14:6 to be "***the*** Way, ***the*** Truth, and ***the*** Life?" There can be no retreat from that truth without abandoning the Gospel altogether, but the church can learn much about the best way to approach this generation. Many pastors are emphasizing visual images in sermons, music styles are being adapted, and stories are being used to teach.

An excellent resource, with twenty-eight knowledgeable contributors, is *Telling the Truth: Evangelizing Postmoderns*, edited by D.A. Carson (Grand Rapids, MI: Zondervan. 2000.) Ravi Zacharias, the well-known apologist for the faith, has also authored and edited an excellent book, *Beyond Opinion: Living the Faith We Defend.* (Nashville, TN: Thomas Nelson. 2007) Periodicals such as *Christianity Today* and *Leadership Journal* also cover this evolving topic in depth.

What we need is a religion that is not only right where we are right, but right where we are wrong.

G. K. Chesterton [10]

Endnotes:

1. Charles Colson, "Doctrine Bears Repeating", *Christianity Today*, (April, 2009), 72.
2. J. I. Packer, quoted in "Doctrine Bears Repeating", *Christianity Today*, (April, 2009), 72.
3. Colson, *Christianity Today*, 72.
4. Peter Kreeft and Ronald K. Tacelli, *Handbook of Christian Apologetics* (Downers Grove, IL: InterVarsity Press, 1994), 252-253.
5. Bjornstad, James, et al. *Christianity, Cults and Religions*. (Torrance, CA: Rose Publishing, Inc., 2008). Pamphlet.
6. Kenneth E. Hagin, *New Thresholds of Faith* (Tulsa: Kenneth Hagin, 1985), 57.
7. Kenneth Copeland, *Now Are We in Christ Jesus* (Fort Worth: KCP Publications, 1980), 17-18, 23-24.
8. Augustine of Hippo, in "Confessions", Chapter 1.
9. Alister E. McGrath, gen. ed., *Zondervan Handbook of Christian Beliefs* (Grand Rapids: Zondervan, 2005), 51, 54.
10. G. K. Chesterton, quoted in David Horton, gen. ed. *The Portable Seminary* (Bloomington, MN: Bethany House Publishers, 2006), 339.

Chapter 4

The Protestant Reformation: How We Got Here

The Protestant Reformation: How We Got Here

> "My situation was that, although an impeccable monk, I stood before God as a sinner troubled in conscience, and I had no confidence that my merit would assuage him. Night and day I pondered until I saw the connection between the justice of God and the statement 'the just shall live by his faith.' Then I grasped that the justice of God is that righteousness by which through grace and sheer mercy God justifies us through faith. Thereupon I felt myself to be reborn and to have gone through open doors into paradise. The whole of Scripture took on a new meaning...This passage of Paul became to me a gate to heaven."[1]
>
> Martin Luther (1483-1586)

Most present-day Christian denominations derive from three very significant events in church history:

The Great Schism which divided the Roman Catholic Church from the Eastern Orthodox Church in 1054 A.D.

The Protestant Reformation, beginning about 1517 A.D.

The Church of England (Anglican) in 1534, splitting from the Roman Catholic Church.

The predominant leader of the Protestant Reformation was **Martin Luther**, a gifted priest and professor at Wittenberg in Germany who became profoundly convinced through his study of the Bible that salvation comes only through faith in Christ Jesus, and who also became adamantly opposed to the rampant corruption in the established Roman Catholic Church. A flashpoint was the sale of "indulgences", a means of raising money for the church by essentially selling forgiveness of sins and release from purgatory. Official positions in the church were also for sale. Luther wrote a list of 95 "theses" or grievances, which he posted on the church door—ushering in a time of great discussion, dispute, and religious revolution. His is a story of great heroism, strong faith, deeply-held convictions, rigid opposition and persecution that eventually led to tremendous revival throughout the western world.

A number of other prominent leaders stepped forward to influence the growing movement, and from these leaders, several "streams" of theological understanding emerged. They are variously described in many resources, but for our purposes in this abbreviated history of denominations, we will consider **five major streams**. Their primary leaders, dates and places of origin, distinctive teachings, and present-day denominations which developed from them are all listed. Most notes about their teachings relate to their views of the nature of man, sin and salvation, and the sacraments. These are presented in order to increase your understanding, not to build fences between sincere believers. These comparative views are charted in sections related to each topic in this book, and are summarized in the Appendix 1.

Five Major Streams of Protestant Theology

Lutherans

- **Dates**: Began about 1517 A.D.
- **Leader:** Martin Luther, and others
- **Place:** Germany, but quickly spread throughout Europe

Luther did not seek separation from Rome, but rather wanted to reform what he viewed as a corrupt system. After refusing to recant, he was excommunicated, his writings were banned, and he was kidnapped by his patron in order to protect him. His writing and teaching continued and ignited a flood of reform that could not be stopped.

- **Distinctive teachings**:

  Man: Total depravity (sinfulness) of man by nature.

  Sin and Salvation: Man is incapable of choosing salvation; his will is fallen or "bound."
  Salvation is by grace alone, through faith alone, in the Word alone!

  Grace: Some believe that God gives "prevenient grace" which enables man to respond to the call of salvation. The idea was defended by Augustine and supported by Psalm 59:10, Romans 8:30, and II Timothy 1:9. The understanding and definition of God's grace has been a subject of study and discussion for centuries, and remains one of the marvelous mysteries of faith.

  Three means of grace: the Word, baptism (water and the Word), the Lord's Supper.

  God predestines those who will be saved, based on His foreknowledge (Rom. 8:29)

  Sanctification is a process and will never be complete until heaven.

  Christians may turn away from their faith and need to be called to repentance.

  Baptism is something God does; infants may be baptized by pouring.

  The Lord's Supper is a means of grace, and Christ's presence is "in, under, between" the elements of bread and wine, often described as the "real presence."

  The "priesthood" of all believers: No intermediary, such as clergy, is necessary.

  The *Augsburg Confession* (1530) and the *Formula of Concord* (1577) define the faith, and *Luther' Catechism* (both the *Large* and the *Small*) is a basis for teaching.

- **Present denominations**:

  There are many, many denominations among the Lutherans—some by location, some by ethnicity, some created through various reform movements, others created by successive mergers. Some are established "state" churches (as in Norway, for example), and others are "free" churches. They are explained in greater depth at the end of this section.

Calvinists (also called "Reformed")

- **Dates:** around 1536
- **Leader**: John Calvin. Ulrich Zwingli led in Switzerland. Later, John Knox started the Calvinist Reformation in Scotland. [2]

> **The Five Points of Calvin** (using the acronym "TULIP"):
>
> **T: Total depravity**: Humans are so sinful that they cannot initiate a return to God.
>
> **U: Unconditional election** (predestination): God chooses who will be saved.
>
> **L: Limited Atonement**: Christ died specifically to save those whom God chose.
>
> **I: Irresistible Grace**: God infallibly draws to Christ those whom He chooses.
>
> **P: Preservation of the Saints** (eternal security): True believers will never fall away from faith, becoming apostate.

- **Place:** Calvin was French, but taught in Geneva
- **Distinctive teachings**:

  Sanctification is a process of becoming Christ-like, rather than an event.

  Baptism of infants is based on view of the covenant. (For a more complete understanding of this position, see Richard Pratt's discussion in *Understanding Four Views of Baptism*, or Daniel R. Hyde's in *Welcome to a Reformed Church.*)

Some groups do not accept all five points of Calvin. Some are "4-Point Calvinists." Classic text is Calvin's "*Institutes of the Christian Religion.*"

- **Present denominations**:
  Presbyterians, some Baptists

Anabaptists

- **Dates:** Around 1525 A.D.
- **Leaders and places**: Early more radical leaders included Thomas Muntzer and Conrad Grebel. Later, Menno Simons (1496-1561) founded the Mennonites in the Netherlands, and Jacob Ammann founded the Amish much later. The Hutterites were founded in Moravia in 1528. William Penn led the Quakers in founding Pennylvania in 1682.
- **Distinctive teachings:**
  "Believers only" baptism of adults only.
  The Lord's Supper is a memorial only.
  Christian behavior and lifestyle is often valued more highly than "correct" doctrine.
  A separatist, non-resistant lifestyle is characteristic of most groups, to varying degrees.
  Some practice communal living.
  Most groups agree on the essentials of God, Jesus, the Holy Spirit, the Trinity, and the Word.
- **Present denominations:**
  Mennonites, Amish, Quakers, Hutterites, some Brethren churches.

Arminians

(Note, this is not a distinct denominational group, but a "stream" of the Reformation.)

- **Dates:** Around 1600
- **Leader:** Jacobus Arminius, a Dutch Reformed theologian, who broke from Calvinism over the Five Points. ("TULIP")
- **Distinctive Teachings**:

Five Points of Arminianism *(in direct contrast to the Five Points of Calvin)* [3]

1. **Free will**: Man has free will, so can accept or reject salvation. Man can cooperate with God.
2. **Conditional election:** God chooses, or "elects", but it is based on His foreknowledge of man's decision.
3. **General atonement**: Jesus' death made atonement for all men.
4. **Resistible grace**: The grace of God can be resisted.
5. **Falling from grace**: Believers can fall away from faith, becoming apostate.

Some groups, among them the Nazarenes, teach "total sanctification" - that believers no longer sin. This is also sometimes referred to as the "holiness" doctrine. According to some recent news reports, some debate and reconsideration is going on within the Nazarenes about the "holiness" doctrine. [4] They also teach that sanctification is a separate post-salvation event or experience, rather than a process.

Sin is defined as only that which is *intentional voluntary transgression*, or *deliberate rebellion*, and thus avoidable.

The Lord's Supper is viewed as only a memorial.

- **Present denominations**:

Methodists (founded by John and Charles Wesley in 1738. The Wesley brothers were Anglican ministers who were active in the Great Awakening movement), Free Methodists, some Baptists, Salvation Army (founded in 1878 by William and Catherine Booth primarily as a ministry to the poor), most Pentecostals, Church of the Nazarene (1908).

Pentecostal/Renewal/Charismatic

- **Dates**: Came much later than the other streams of the Reformation. Often seen as originating with the Azusa Street revivals of 1906.
- **Leader and Place:** The Azusa Street revivals in Los Angeles were led by William Seymour, but the movement quickly spread around the globe.
- **Distinctive teachings**:

Emphasis on baptism of the Holy Spirit as a post-conversion experience, usually accompanied by speaking in tongues.

Most doctrinal positions are Arminian regarding man, sin, and salvation.

Some followers are organized within denominations, while others are associated as renewal movements within other denominations.

There is strong emphasis on world missions, and the Pentecostal movement is growing very quickly worldwide because of its aggressive evangelistic efforts.

- **Present denominations**:

Assemblies of God, Church of God, International Church of the Foursquare Gospel (founded by Aimee Semple McPherson, with an emphasis on healing), Calvary Chapel (founded by Chuck Smith in California) , Vineyard Ministries International (early leader John Wimber, in 1982, with strong emphasis on "signs and wonders").

Other large denominations

- **Baptist**

Trace their roots to John Smythe and the Puritans in 1612. Most of the Baptist denominations are firmly evangelical, strong on inerrancy of Scripture and essential doctrines of man, God, the Trinity, and salvation. Baptism is by immersion of adults only. The Lord's Supper is viewed as memorial only. The Southern Baptist Convention is conservative and is the largest Protestant denomination in the USA. American Baptists and National Baptists are mainline churches. Most are Calvinist/Reformed in their doctrinal distinctives.

- **Congregational**

Began as house churches in England who were separating from the Church of England over doctrinal issues. They were forced into exile and fled to Plymouth on the *Mayflower* in 1620 where they were called "Pilgrims." Present denominations include the United Church of Christ, a very liberal, mainline body; The National Association of Congregational Christian Churches, and the Conservative Congregational Christian Conference ("4 C's") which is evangelical.

- **Churches of Christ**

Began with revival movements in the early 1800's in Kentucky. The "Churches of

Christ" are conservative, and the "Disciples of Christ" is the mainline, more liberal body. They hold a variety of views on the infallibility of Scripture, and some essential doctrines. Baptism is immersion of believers only, and the Lord's Supper is symbolic memorial. Some groups forbid the use of instrumental music in worship.

- **Evangelical Covenant Church, Evangelical Free Church of America**

Both groups have their roots in the Free Church tradition of Scandinavia, breaking with the Lutheran State churches there. They are firmly evangelical. The Evangelical Free Church accepts both infant and believers' baptism according to a compromise reached in 1950, allowing pastors and members to hold and practice either view. [5]

- **Christian and Missionary Alliance**

Founded by A.B. Simpson, a faith-healing evangelist of the late nineteenth century. It is strongly evangelical and historically very active in world mission outreach.

The Lutherans in America

Lutherans came to America largely from Germany and from the Scandinavian countries, where Lutheranism was the state religion. At one time there were actually 150 Lutheran bodies in the United States! They organized themselves along either ethnic (thus the Norwegian Lutheran Church, or the German Lutheran Church) or theological lines. Some were heavily influenced by the Pietist renewal movement begun by Philip Jacob Spener in the mid 17th century. Spener wrote a book meaning *Pious Desires*, the subtitle of which was *Heartfelt Yearnings for the God-pleasing Improvement of the True Evangelical Church.* He encouraged personal study of the Bible, small group Bible studies, devout Christian living and discipleship. Some of these synods were more theologically conservative than others; some were liturgical in worship style and others practiced low-church worship; some were more hierarchal, while others emphasized the priesthood of all believers and encouraged active participation of lay people.

As time went on, many of the ethnic groups began to merge into larger bodies, and at each merger new groups were formed in protest. Charts which map this evolution of Lutheranism in America are complex, but can be found in sources such as *What's Going on Among the Lutherans*? by Patsy A. Leppien and J. Kincaid Smith (Milwaukee, WI: Northwestern Publishing House. 1992). In the first years of this 21st century, there is increasing turmoil and fallout among the mainline Lutheran denominations over the issue of homosexual practice, gay marriage and ordination of homosexuals. The underlying issue, however, is the inerrancy of Scripture.

The Three Largest Lutheran Denominations in America

Note: Figures are the most recent available from The Association of Religious Data Archives (www.thearda.com). Sources of additional information include: *Handbook of Denominations in the United State*s 12th Edition. Frank S. Mead, Samuel S. Hill, Craig D. Atwood (Nashville: Abingdon Press. 2005). and *The Lutheran Handbook II.* Barbara S. Wilson and Arlene Flancher, editors. (Minneapolis: Augsburg Fortress. 2007).

The Evangelical Lutheran Church in America (ELCA)
Headquarters: Chicago, Illinois
Congregations: 10,396 in 2008
Founded: 1988

- Membership: 4,633,887 in 2008
- The ELCA resulted from the merger of the American Lutheran Church (ALC), Lutheran Church in America (LCA), and Association of Evangelical Lutheran Churches (AELC). Both the ALC (in 1960) and the LCA (in 1962) had been mergers of German and Scandinavian synods. The AELC had been a break-away from the Lutheran Church-Missouri Synod in 1976 over the issue of the authority and interpretation of Scripture.
- Its publishing arm is Augsburg Fortress Press.
- It has a formal relationship of full communion with the Presbyterian Church (U.S.A.), Reformed Church in America, the United Church of Christ, and the Episcopal Church.

The Lutheran Church—Missouri Synod (LCMS)
Headquarters: St. Louis, Missouri
Congregations: 6,123 in 2008
Founded: 1847

- Membership: 2,337,349 in 2008
- Considered more conservative than the larger ELCA, produces the well-known "Lutheran Hour" radio broadcast, and its publishing arm is Concordia Publishing House.
- Operates twelve universities and seminaries in North America as well as hundreds of elementary and secondary schools.

The Wisconsin Evangelical Lutheran Synod (WELS)
Headquarters: Milwaukee, Wisconsin
Congregations: 1,286 in 2008
Founded: 1850

- Membership: 390,213 in 2008
- It is a confessional Lutheran church with strong emphasis on the inerrancy of Scripture. It supports extensive missions throughout the world, and a college and seminary in the United States.

Others Major Lutheran Denominations in America

American Association of Lutheran Churches (AALC)
Headquarters: Minneapolis, Minnesota
Congregations: 70 in 2008
Founded: 1988

- Membership: 16,000 in 2008
- Formed by pastors and laity of the former American Lutheran Church (ALC) who wished to stay out of the 1988 merger that formed the ELCA.
- It is strongly evangelical, firm on inerrancy of Scripture, and committed to evangelism and missions.

Association of Free Lutheran Congregations (AFLC)
Headquarters: Plymouth, Minnesota
Congregations: 274 in 2008
Founded: 1962

- Membership: 43,477 in 2008
- Formed by congregations of the Lutheran Free Church who rejected the merger with what became the ALC in 1962. Its roots were in the revival movement in Scandinavia in the late 19th century; it is strongly evangelical and firm on the inerrancy of Scripture.

Church of the Lutheran Confession
Headquarters: Eau Claire, Wisconsin
Congregations: 87
Founded; 1960

- Membership: 14,752 in 2008
- Formed in separation from mergers of several synods, holding strongly to inerrancy.

Church of the Lutheran Brethren of America (CLBA)
Headquarters: Fergus Falls, Minnesota
Congregations: 116 in 2008
Founded: 1900

- Membership: 15, 050 in 2011 (parishioners)
- Rather than forming as a splinter group from a merger of ethnic churches, the CLBA had its roots in the pietistic renewal movement in Norway. New immigrants to the United States with a zeal for personal living faith and passion for world mission formed an independent Lutheran body made up of autonomous congregations. They maintain world missions in Chad, Cameroon, Taiwan and Japan, a junior high, high school (Hillcrest Lutheran Academy) and seminary in Fergus Falls, Minnesota, and Faith and Fellowship Press.

Two Very Recently-formed Lutheran Denominations

Lutheran Congregations in Mission for Christ (LCMC)
Formed in a Lutheran renewal movement
Headquarters: Canton, Michigan
Congregations: 695 in 2012

North American Lutheran Church (NALC)
Formed in 2010 in protest against policies of the Evangelical Church in America (ELCA).
Headquarters: Hilliard, Ohio
Congregations: 300 in 2012

The CLBA Among the Lutherans – Distinctive Views

Church government: Congregations are autonomous, but conform to a Statement of Faith, and pastors are ordained by the synod.

Style of worship: Non-liturgical, with emphasis on participation of lay people.

The Bible: Firmly committed to the inerrancy of Scripture.

Conversion: Stress the need for evangelism to those both inside and outside of the church, as children need to be brought to a conscious experience of living faith, and believers can fall away and need to be called to repentance.

Pietism: Emphasize godly living, a personal relationship with Christ and growing faith.

Confirmation: Confirmation is viewed as completion of instruction in the foundational truths of the faith as taught in *Luther's Small Catechism.* It does not bring automatic membership in the congregation or include a vow to follow Christ.

Church membership: Granted on the basis of a statement of personal faith. The church is seen as a body of true believers while acknowledging some hypocrites may be among the believers.

Social issues: Conservative on social issues such as abortion, the sanctity of marriage, and homosexuality. CLBA has official statements on these issues which may be obtained through the website, www.clba.org.

Ordination of pastors/elders*:* CLBA is complementarian, viewing women as equal in value with men but called to different roles and responsibilities in the church, so women are not ordained.

Mission Statement—Church of the Lutheran Brethren

In response to God's person and grace, we worship Him with everything we are in Christ, serve one another in Christian love and share the Gospel of Jesus Christ with all people.

Vision Statement—Church of the Lutheran Brethren

We see God stirring in our church a fresh passion to reach beyond our own comfort to all people among whom God places us. We embrace God's mission to bring the life-changing Gospel to unreached people in Asia and Africa, and we sense God convicting us to more intentionally reach out to people who live in our midst in North America as well. [6]

Core Values—Church of the Lutheran Brethren

Introduction: The Church of the Lutheran Brethren has adopted a *Statement of Faith* based upon and drawn from Holy Scripture. It states in precise language what we as a church, under the guidance of the Holy Spirit and in community with each other, have declared to be our common belief. It is our charter, our constitution, and our most fundamental document. From this statement flows another one, a *Statement of Core Values*. In it we state our passions and our desires. As the *Statement of Faith* declares our core beliefs, our *Statement of Core Values* explains how we desire to live out our faith.

The Bible is central in our congregations and in our households. The Word of God is the focus of our worship services, the textbook for our teaching ministries, and the foundation of our daily lives. Whether we are preaching, teaching, singing or just talking, we want to be people of the Word.

The Gospel is our treasure and our joy. We want the Good News of God's grace to us in Jesus Christ to be the centerpiece of our mission. All people need the Gospel. God's children need to hear it again and again. The Good News is God's power, which saves us, draws us together and motivates us for service.

We revere God's Law. The Law of God cannot save us, but it is necessary for our salvation. We need to see our sin and be driven to the cross of Christ for forgiveness. We need to be reminded that we cannot earn God's love or merit His blessings. We also need the ethical guidance which God's Law gives. We dare not make up our own morality.

The Word and the Sacraments are God's precious means of grace. The Word teaches us, Baptism washes us, and the Lord's Supper nourishes us. In our sacramental life together we are brought again and again to the crucified and risen Jesus Christ, who alone is the source of our salvation.

We cherish the love and fellowship of God's people. We need each other. We need the spiritual gifts, which the Holy Spirit imparts to His people. We experience God's peace as we worship and work together, forgive one another, and bear one another's burdens.

We long for people to trust in Jesus Christ as Savior and Lord, to come to know Him in a personal way. We are called by the love of Christ to share His Gospel. Our mission is as local as our neighborhood and as universal as the whole world.

We seek to be people of prayer. Whether in public worship, small groups or in our personal lives, we want prayer to be foundational. Prayer supports and propels us in our mission. We desire that prayer be as essential in our ministries as breath is to our physical life.[7]

The Church's One Foundation

Samuel J. Stone, Samuel S. Wesley, 1864

The Church's one foundation is Jesus Christ her Lord;
She is His new creation by water and the word.
From heaven He came and sought her to be His holy Bride;
With His own blood He bought her and for her life He died.

Elect from every nation, yet one o'er all the earth;
Her charter of salvation: One Lord, One faith, One birth;
One holy Name she blesses, partakes one holy food;
And to one hope she presses with every grace endued.[8]

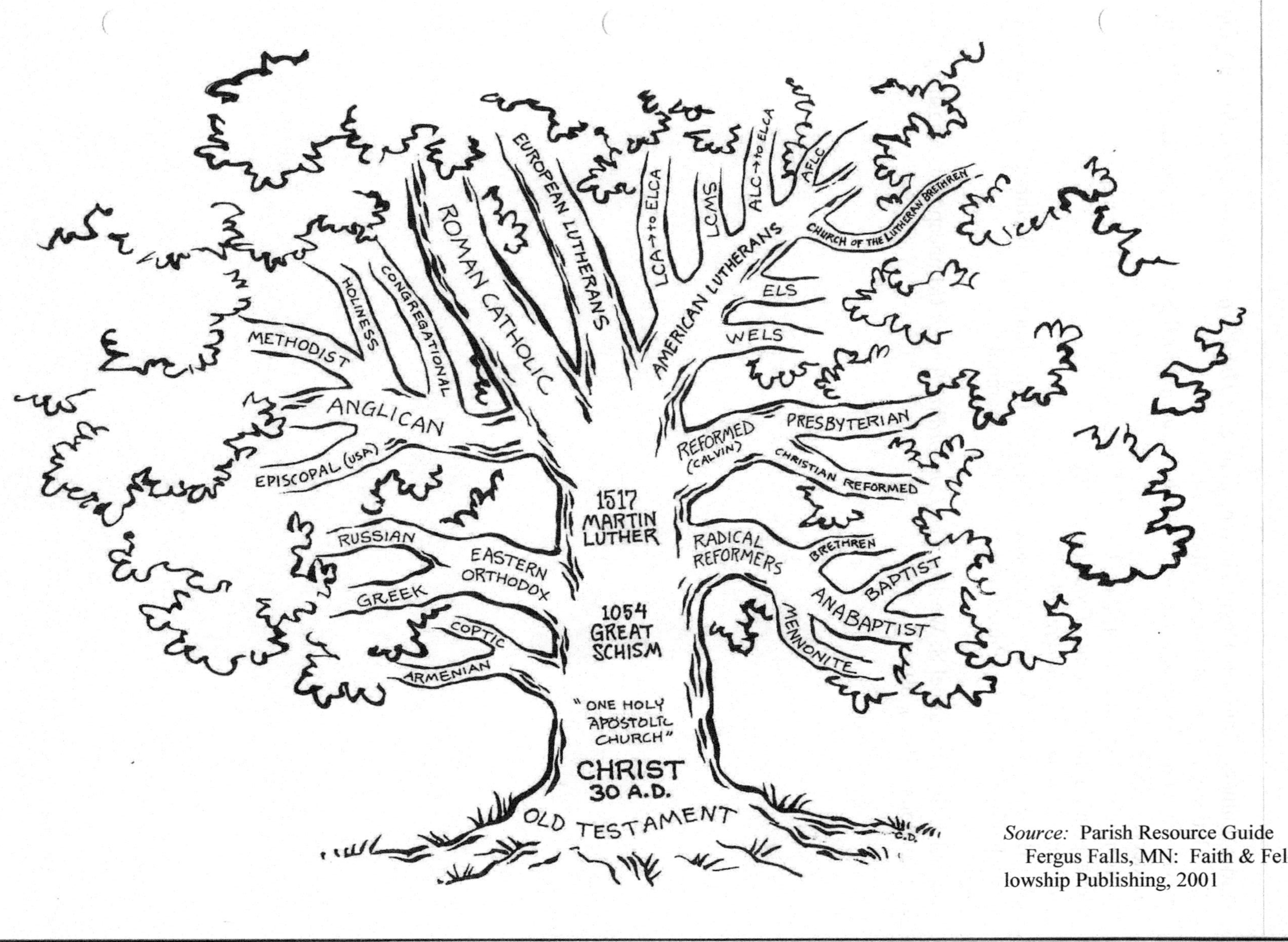

Source: Parish Resource Guide
Fergus Falls, MN: Faith & Fellowship Publishing, 2001

Endnotes:

---

1. Martin Luther, quoted in David Horton, gen. ed., *The Portable Seminary* (Bloomington, MN: Bethany House Publishers, 2006), 474.
2. Wayne Grudem, *Systematic Theology, An Introduction to Biblical Doctrine* (Grand Rapids: Zondervan, 1994), 679.
3. "Reformation Timeline" (Torrance, CA: RW Research, Inc., 2006). Pamphlet.
4. News posting in *Christianity Today* (July, 2007), 17.
5. Grudem, *Systematic Theology*, 983-984.
6. "We Believe– Core Values Statement, Church of the Lutheran Brethren" (Fergus Falls, MN: Faith & Fellowship Publishing, rev. 2007). Pamphlet.
7. Ibid.
8. Samuel J. Stone, Samuel S. Wesley, *The Concordia Hymnal* (Minneapolis: Augsburg Publishing House, 1933), 80.

Chapter 5

Salvation: Man's Plight and God's Solution

Salvation: Man's Plight and God's Solution

A white rose on the altar...

That has been the long-standing traditional way of celebrating the new life of an individual who has come to personal living faith in Christ Jesus that week at Our Redeemer's Lutheran Brethren Church, in Minot, North Dakota. It is a rare Sunday that the vase is empty. Usually the new believer is not identified, but the congregation takes time to praise the work of the Lord in this life, and to rejoice together.

On a recent Sunday when my friend joined in worship, there were three roses. As the pastor noted them, a young man seated in the large group of hearing-impaired worshipers sprang to his feet and in large, enthusiastic gestures signed "It was ME!"

There was applause, and there were tears of joy!

And there was joy in heaven...

Born again...
Converted...
Committed to Christ...
Becoming a believer in Christ...
Asking Jesus into your heart...
Being saved...
Accepting Christ as your personal Savior

Scripture uses many terms and word pictures—and so do we—to describe the experience of "conscious, living faith" which must occur as one matures, whether baptized as an infant or not. It may occur suddenly or over a period of time in response to the Gospel. It may grow from the seed of faith planted when God's grace was extended to us in baptism. It is a mystery, but we see its evidence in lives transformed. We see it in people who've been very religious but have had no living faith or relationship to Jesus. And we see it in people who've rejected Him entirely, living lives far from faith, whom God has graciously intercepted, called to repentance, and saved. Sometimes it has been very dramatic, and sometimes it has been very quiet.

Though there is much about salvation that is mystery, Scripture is very clear about many things:

- It must occur. Salvation through Jesus Christ is absolutely essential, because by nature man is fallen, lost, and estranged from God. (Acts 4:12)
- Man cannot save himself, but God provides all that is needed, by His grace alone, through faith alone. (Ephesians 2:9)
- Salvation is available to all. (John 3:16; Acts 2:21)
- God's offer of salvation must be believed and accepted by faith. (John 1:12)
- God will not reject anyone who comes to Him in faith. (John 6:37)

What does this look like? What is sin? On what basis may we be saved from sin? Is salvation available to everyone? Does God choose who will be saved? How do I live as a believer? Can I choose to live for God? Can a believer ever turn away from faith and be lost?

Sin: Is the human race really lost?

IT IS WRITTEN:

- Isaiah 53:6, "We all, like sheep, have gone astray, each of us has turned to his own way; and the Lord has laid on him the iniquity of us all."
- Isaiah 64:6, "All of us have become like one who is unclean, and all our righteous acts are like filthy rags."
- Romans 3:23, "All have sinned and fall short of the glory of God."
- Ephesians 2:1-3, "As for you, you were dead in your transgressions and sins, in which you used to live when you followed the ways of this world and of the ruler of the kingdom of the air, the spirit who is now at work in those who are disobedient. All of us also lived among them at one time, gratifying the cravings of our sinful nature and following its desires and thoughts. Like the rest, we were by nature objects of wrath."

"We must not suppose that even if we succeeded in making everyone nice we should have saved their souls...A world of nice people, content in their own niceness, looking no further, turned away from God, would be just as desperately in need of salvation as a miserable world...for mere improvement is not redemption...God became man to turn creatures into sons: not simply to produce better men of the old kind but to produce a new kind of man. It is not like teaching a horse to jump better and better, but like turning a horse into a winged creature.
A fallen man is not simply an imperfect creature who needs improvement: he is a rebel who must lay down his arms." [1]
- C.S. Lewis

God's creation was good and perfect. (Genesis 1:31) Mankind had been created in the image of God:

They had a desire to do God's will; harmony with God.

They had a conscience filled with peace and joy; harmony within.

They had an understanding of God and His works; harmony with nature. In this state of innocence, they had free wills and could live without sinning. God desired a growing relationship with humanity based upon love and choice. This relationship would become stronger and be eternal.

BUT, man fell into sin when Adam and Eve were tempted by Satan and chose to disobey God. Adam and Eve passed this sin nature on to their children, so that they were all now born sinners. This is called "original" or "inherited sin." All men are also guilty of actual sinful deeds which arise from our sinful nature. As is often said, "We sin because *we are sinners*—we are not sinners because *we sin*." It is our nature, and it places us under God's condemnation: "The wages of sin is death…" (Romans 6:23)

"The basic nature of sin is unbelief. The path from God is the opposite of the path back to God. If the basic nature of sin were disobedience, the way back to God would be the way of obedience. If the path away from God is the path of unbelief, the path back to God is the way of faith." [2]
- Omar Gjerness

Man's lost state:

Professor Omar Gjerness writes in *Knowing Good From Evil,* "Christian ethics is pessimistic ethics. It declares that all of mankind is born under obligation to keep a perfect moral law. The Bible says 'Be holy as I am holy.' It also declares, 'The soul that sins shall die.' It declares that no one except Jesus Christ has ever kept the law. One conclusion is inevitable. Mankind under the law is under the curse of God. His ethical situation is hopeless. He can try to approximate morality, and under social righteousness can achieve a measure of righteousness and morality, but he can never achieve what God demands. Our conclusion must be that man under the law, before regeneration, is cursed and helpless before the Almighty God." [3]

> ***"This is most certainly true…"***
> **111. What is sin?**
> Sin is everything that is contrary to God's holy law and includes both inherited and actual sin. (I John 3:4)
> **112. What is inherited sin (often called original sin)?**
> Inherited sin is the inborn tendency to wickedness, deep corruption, and evil inclination of my human nature, with no power to believe in God or save myself by my good works. (Ps. 51:5, Rom. 5:12)
> **113. What is actual sin?**
> Actual sin is all evil thoughts and desires, words and deeds which come from inherited sin.
> **117. What judgment does God pronounce upon you because of your failure to obey His law perfectly?**
> My judgment is eternal death. (Gal. 3:10)
> **118. What help, then, is there for you?**
> I may be saved through the grace of Jesus Christ offered to me in the Gospel. (John 3:16,17)
> *-Explanation of Luther's Small Catechism*

Comparative Views of Sin:

Lutheran	Arminian	Calvinist
Man is a slave to sin, and has no free will. His will is incapable of cooperating with God. God's grace enables man to accept the Gospel.	Man is thoroughly infected by sin, but has free will. Man's will is capable of cooperating with God, a benefit of the atonement.	Man is enslaved to sin and has no free will. Man's will is not capable of cooperating with God.
Man is totally depraved	Depravity is extensive, but could be worse.	Total depravity of man
Sin is transgression of God's Law	Sin is a "voluntary transgression of a known law." It is intentional	Sin is transgression of God's Law.

Besides disobedience of the 10 Commandments, given in Exodus 20, a number of other Scriptures list specific sins. It is useful to study them, to examine one's self , to repent and confess these sins to a forgiving Savior (Acts. 3:19).

Romans 1:28-32 I Corinthians 6:9-10
Galatians 5:19-21 2 Timothy 3:1-5

For further study see: *The Christian Faith* (Kolb); *Systematic Theology* (Grudem), *The Portable Seminary* (Horton); *We Believe* (Ysteboe) *Handbook of Christian Beliefs* (McGrath).; *Five Views of Law and Gospel* (Gundry). See Bibliography.

Justification: On what basis may I be saved from my sin?

One day many years ago in northern Minnesota, my grandmother, Bertha Wold, was covered in flour, busily baking bread for her large family. Her heart was heavy because of the severe illness of her young son-in-law who lived just down the street and who had no apparent faith in the Lord Jesus. She was suddenly convicted that she herself must go and speak to him—so she dusted herself off, tucked her Bible under her arm and walked to his home. There she read one verse only to him: "God made him who had no sin to be sin for us, so that in him we might become the righteousness of God." (2 Cor. 5:21) God opened his heart to understand the Gospel truth of the atonement: Christ had paid the penalty for his sin. He believed that, and shortly was called home to meet His Savior face to face!

"Where there is the Word of the God who makes promises, there must necessarily be the faith of the person who accepts those promises. It is clear that the beginning of our salvation is a faith which clings to the Word of a promising God who, without any effort on our part, in free and unmerited mercy goes before us and offers us a word of promise."[4]
-Martin Luther

So how did God provide a way out for His beloved creation that had fallen so tragically into sin? The Bible uses many terms for this:

10 Terms You Should Know:

Atonement A spiritual word of oneness with God,
Based on what Jesus did on the cross.

Redemption An economic word for payment,
Jesus paid for our sins.

Justification A legal word for erase,
As if my sin never happened.

Forgiveness An emotional word of release,
My sin has been taken from me; I am free of guilt.

Deliverance A political word for freedom.
I am *free from* bondage to sin and *free to* worship and serve God.

Salvation A medical word for health,
A healthy relationship with God.
Also often thought of as "rescue."[5]

Conversion To acknowledge with repentance my sin and my need and by faith believe that Jesus Christ has taken my guilt, forgiven me, and become my substitute.[6]

Faith Personal belief and trust in a person or an idea, such that loss will be inevitable if the object of faith proves untrustworthy. Christian faith in Jesus Christ is therefore more than an intellectual assent to beliefs: it is personal commitment to Jesus.[7]

Repentance A complete turning around, from any way other than Jesus' way, to following Jesus. It may be accompanied by feelings of remorse, but the key is the actual change of heart and life.[8]

Grace The unmerited—unearned—favor of God. Often described as "God's Riches At Christ's Expense."

The hands that should discard me hold wounds that tell me, "Come!"[9]

-Keith and Kristyn Getty in their hymn, "*Beneath the Cross*"

Two aspects of salvation: Justification and Regeneration.

- **Justification** is an *action of God which takes place in heaven* . It is a statement, declaration, or verdict which God makes, in which a person's sins are removed and he is credited with Christ's righteousness.
- **Regeneration** is an *act of God which takes place in man*, in which he is given a new nature and God's image is restored in him. The Holy Spirit also begins to live in him.

This is most certainly true…

222. What is justification?

Justification is the gracious act of God by which He, for Christ's sake, acquits me (declares me not guilty), a repentant and believing sinner of my sin and guilt, credits me with Christ's righteousness, and looks upon me, in Christ, as though I had never sinned. (Eph. 2:8; II Corinthians 5:21; Isaiah 53:5)

223. **What gifts come to you because of justification**?

Because of justification I have received:

1. Adoption as God's child (Rom. 8:15, 17)
2. Peace with God
3. Joy in suffering
4. Hope
5. The love of God
6. The Holy Spirit (Romans 5:1-5)

224. Why should the church always hold and teach this doctrine of justification by grace alone?

The church must always hold and teach this doctrine because it is the chief doctrine of the Christian religion; it distinguishes the Christian religion from false religion which teaches salvation by works; it gives enduring comfort to the repentant sinner; and it gives all glory to God.

225. For whose sake does God forgive you your sins?

God does not forgive my sins because I deserve it, but only because of what Christ did on the cross, when His blood paid for the sins of the whole world. (I John 2:1, 2)

226. What happens to you when your sins are forgiven?

When God forgives me my sins for the sake of Jesus Christ, He blots them all out, and I do not have them any more. (Isaiah 43:25; Isaiah 1:18)

227. Why is this such good news?

This is good news because my sins stand between me and God, and without this forgiveness I would spend eternity in hell without God. (John 3:36; Romans 8:1)

Explanation of Luther's Small Catechism

Who initiates salvation?

Lutherans—and most Protestants—are emphatic in their conviction that God ***alone*** initiates and accomplishes salvation: man is totally lost and cannot do anything to save himself. Martin Luther was once asked what we contributed to our salvation. He replied, "*Sin and resistance*!". Five critical truths ("*solas*") about salvation, proclaimed during the Reformation are:

- The Word Alone (*Sola Scriptura*)
- For the Glory of God Alone (*Soli Deo Gloria*)
- By Christ's Work Alone (*Solo Christo*)
- Salvation by Grace Alone (*Sola Gratia*)

Is salvation available to everyone?

"Everyone who calls on the name of the Lord will be saved." (Romans 10:13)

"All that the Father gives me will come to me, and whoever comes to me I will never drive away." (John 6:37)

"God so loved the world that He gave His one and only Son, [in NIV, or 'only begotten son' in KJV] that whoever believes in him shall not perish but have eternal life." (John 3:16)

Comparative Views of the Atonement

Some denominations teach that the atonement of Christ was only for those whom God chose before time. (See the doctrine of Predestination, p.78) This view is called "*limited atonement.*" Lutherans believe that God provided fully for the salvation of all people.

Lutheran	Arminian	Calvinist
Christ died for all	Christ died for all	Christ died for the elect (chosen)
Atonement is not limited to the elect	Atonement is for all men even those who go lost.	Atonement is for the elect only

Comparative Views of Salvation

Eastern Orthodox "What is necessary in order to please God and to save one's own soul? In the first place, a knowledge of the true God, and a right faith in Him; in the second place, a life according to faith, and good works." (*The Longer Catechism of the Eastern Church, Question 3)*

Lutheran "Our churches teach that people cannot be justified before God by their own strength, merits, or works. People are freely justified for Christ's sake, through faith, when they believe that they are received into favor and that their sins are forgiven for Christ's sake." (*Augsburg Confession IV 2*)

Reformed/Presbyterian "Those whom God effectually calleth He also freely justifieth; not by infusing righteousness into them, but by pardoning their sins...for Christ's sake alone." (*The Westminster Confession of Faith XI:I)*

Baptist "We believe that the great gospel blessing which Christ secures to such as believe in him is Justification; that Justification includes the pardon of sin, and the promise of eternal life on principles of righteousness; that it is bestowed...solely through faith in the Redeemer's blood." (*The New Hampshire Baptist Confession V)*

Wesleyan/Methodist "We are accounted righteous before God only for the merit of our Lord and Savior Jesus Christ by faith, and not for our own works or deservings." (*Methodist Articles of Religion IX*)

Liberal "The traditional soteriology [doctrine of sin] presupposed the historicity of Adam's fall and started from the assumption that mankind needs to be saved primarily from the taint inherited from Adam. But modern anthropology has discredited this way of determining the nature of man and of sin." (Gerald Birney Smith in *A Guide to the Study of the Christian Religion*, p. 519)

Source: *Justification and Sanctification,* Korey Maas [10]

The Way of Salvation: How Does it Occur?

- ☐ I grew up in a Christian home and have always believed in God.
- ☐ I am active in my church, and support it with my gifts and service.
- ☐ I am a spiritual person: I worship, read the Bible, and pray.
- ☐ I have lived a moral life and try to practice the Golden Rule in all my ways.
- ☐ All of the above

A Christian would endorse all these as very desirable, but in truth, they are not what makes one a Christian. ***What then must I do?***

- Acknowledge that what the Word of God says about all people is also true of you. "*No one* is good, not one of us. For all of us have sinned and fallen short of God's glory . . . And the wage sin pays is death." (Romans 3:12, 23; 6:23)
- We are all born with a spiritual disease called sin that afflicts us on the deepest level of our personalities. It poisons everything we do, so that despite our best efforts, we cannot please God. The harder we try, the greater is the awareness of our guilt and alienation from Him, and the fear of His judgment. (Romans 7:7-23)
- ***Here is the good news!*** What we cannot do for ourselves, God did for us through His Son Jesus Christ. Jesus took our place and lived the God-pleasing life on earth we could not live. He then offered His life in death as just payment for our guilt. In raising Him from the dead, God said, "I'm satisfied!" (Romans 8:1-4)
- When believing this good news, we acknowledge our sin, and open our hearts to receive Jesus Christ and the free gift of all He did for us; God forgives our sin, declares us His friends, and sends His Spirit to live in us. We will then confess in truth, "I am a Christian!"
- ***Then what?*** As Christians, we live, not depending on how we may feel at the moment, but by faith, which is simply taking God at His Word. We no longer live to earn God's acceptance. Instead, we live to express the reality of what He has so graciously made us—***His own children!*** (Romans 12:1, 2)

-Rev. Dan Lazicki, in the welcome brochure of Grace Lutheran Church, Lynnwood, Washington. Used by permission.

I sought the Lord, and afterward I knew

Hymn, by George W. Chadwick

I sought the Lord, and afterward I knew
He moved my soul to seek Him, seeking me;
It was not I that found, O Savior true;
No, I was found of Thee.

Thou didst reach forth thy hand and mine enfold;
I walked and sank not on the storm-vexed sea;
'Twas not so much that I on Thee took hold,
As Thou, dear Lord, on me.

I find, I walk, I love; but O the whole
Of love is but my answer, Lord, to Thee!
For Thou wert long beforehand with my soul
Always Thou lovedst me. [11]

> *Only forgiveness without reason can match sin without excuse.*
> -Edwin H. Robertson

There is much confusion about an individual's *WILL* and his involvement in his salvation. Lutherans believe that man's will is bound: that his only capacity is to resist God. However through God's grace he is enabled to cease resisting, to respond to God's offer of salvation. Some call this work of God "prevenient" grace, described by Dr. Roger Olson as, "grace that convicts, calls, illumines, and enables."[12] Our language makes it difficult to express this without making it appear to be our work, which it emphatically is *NOT*. Think about it this way:

If I buy you a gift, wrap it, address it to you, knock on your door and extend the gift to you—and you open your hand and receive it, that certainly does not mean that you gave it to yourself, that is, that you worked for it, and deserved it. That is foolishness! You only responded—you opened your naturally-clenched hands and received what was offered. Or, you R.S.V.P'd to the invitation, to use another word picture. Scripture is full of words to describe this response: believe, repent, come, follow me, trust, accept, choose.

Many Lutherans have a far more "passive" view of how salvation occurs. For an extensive study of this position, see Steven P. Mueller in *Called to Believe*, chapter 10, or Robert Kolb in *The Christian Faith*, chapter 10.

Peter Kreeft, in *Handbook of Christian Apologetics* described the process of becoming a Christian this way. Never forget, though, that this is ALL in response to God's grace!

1. **Mental belief**. You cannot seek or deal with a Person you do not believe exists. (Hebrews 11:6, "Without faith it is impossible to please God, because anyone who comes to him must believe that he exists and that he rewards those who earnestly seek Him.")
2. **Repentance from sin.** Not just feeling guilty, but turning around.
3. **Saving faith**. Receiving Christ as Savior and Lord of your soul, your life, your destiny.
4. **Traveling down His way**. Actually living the Christian life.

These last two necessarily go together. In three, the tree of Christ's life is planted in you; in four, it bears fruit. (James 1:25, "Faith without works is dead.") [13]

> *"No one will launch a boat thinking the sea is only a myth; but believing in the sea is not sufficient to become a sailor."* -Peter Kreeft

Professor M.E. Sletta, long-time dogmatics professor at Lutheran Brethren Seminary in Fergus Falls, Minnesota, listed these elements in salvation.

The call (including awakening and illumination), that is, God's offer of salvation. "The call is the activity of the Holy Spirit by which he awakens a dead sinner through the Word of God to see his lost condition, and by which he invites him and makes him willing to accept God's saving grace in Christ."

Conversion (including contrition, repentance, and faith), that is, our answer to God's call. Sletta's definition of conversion: "It is the choice the sinner makes when he becomes willing to submit to God's sentence of condemnation and plead guilty, and in despair over his hopeless condition, to cast himself as a lost sinner at the feet of Christ...We human beings repent and believe the gospel, but it is God's Holy Spirit that prompts us to do so."

Justification and regeneration. After saying that justification is a change in God's way of looking at us and regeneration is a change in our way of looking at God, Sletta gives these definitions: "Justification is the great cause in the heart of God in heaven declaring a believing sinner to be saved from his sins and righteous in Christ as his adopted child; regeneration is the great effect by the Holy Spirit in the heart of man on earth by which he becomes a new creature." [14]

This is most certainly true…

205. Is it enough for you to know all these things about Christ and consider them to be true in order to be saved?

No, the Holy Spirit must teach me to know Christ as my Savior from sin. (John 3:5-8; I Corinthians 12:3)

218. What is a true and living faith in Jesus Christ?

When I as a repentant sinner receive Jesus Christ as my only Savior from sin, death, and the power of the devil, and find refuge in Him and confidently rely upon Him, then I have a true and living faith in Jesus Christ. Furthermore, a true and living faith will show itself by good works. (Matthew 5:1; James 2:17; Ephesians 2:10)

-Explanation to Luther's Small Catechism

What part does a believer play in his salvation?

1. Some teach that the human *cooperates* (shares the work) with God. This is called **Synergism.**
2. Some teach that the human will is *controlled by God's will.* This is **Predestination**.
3. Lutherans (and others) believe that grace comes to the unsaved *creating faith in God's promises and provision of salvation.* This is salvation by grace through faith. They teach that salvation is *all of God.* This is **Monergism.**
4. Some teach that people can *resist the grace of God* that is extended to them, while others teach that *His grace is not resistible.* It follows, then, that if His grace is not resistible, those whom God has chosen in predestination will be saved and will never be lost.

Lutheran	Arminian	Calvinist
Monergistic: God alone saves	Synergistic: God and man co-operate in salvation	Monergistic: God alone saves
God's grace is resistible	God's grace is resistible	God's grace is irresistible

Election (also called Predestination):

Does God choose who will be saved and who will be lost?

By far the most difficult doctrine regarding salvation is the doctrine of Election, also called Predestination. It addresses the issue: If it is God's will for all men to be saved and to know the truth (I Timothy 2:4) and He is sovereign, why are not all people saved? Did God decide before time began that some would be "chosen" for salvation, while others were not, that is, in effect they were then chosen to be damned? Does that sound like the actions of God whom we know to be totally good, totally fair, totally just? The verse, among many, which is often cited is this:

"We know that in everything God works for good with those who love him, who are called according to his purpose. For those whom he foreknew he also predestined to be conformed to the image of his Son, in order that he might be the first-born among many brethren. And those whom he predestined he also called; and those whom he called he also justified; and those whom he justified he also glorified." (Romans 8:28-30)

Because God exists outside of a timeline (or above it, as C.S. Lewis observes), but we are bound to time, it is impossible for us to imagine a "process" that does not include a sequence of action. However, because this is an area of disagreement among Protestant denominations, we will include quotations from the Lutheran viewpoint as well as the Calvinist and Arminian ones. For further study, read Wayne Grudem's careful discussion of the topic in *Systematic Theology*. Though he himself is of the Calvinist viewpoint he takes pains to present other views fairly. It would also be a great discussion to have with your own pastor!

From the Lutheran, Robert Kolb in *The Christian Faith*:

"Martin Luther understood God's unconditioned choice of his people as a word of Gospel. It was good news that our being God's children stands completely apart from anything in us. In us uncertainty reigns. Only God gives assurance that we are safe in God's hands and shall remain so. At the same time Luther steadfastly resisted the temptation to pierce the mystery of election and answer the question why some are saved and not others. Instead, he focused on the specific and immediate need of the sinner. To the secure sinner the Law—not the doctrine of election—must be presented. Secure sinners need to hear God's word of Law, which holds them responsible for their own misdeeds and their own denial of God. Only to the broken and despairing sinner can the words of comfort come, which the doctrine of election is designed to bring, according to Luther."[15]

Note: Lutherans teach that election is ***conditional upon faith***, which is a gift of God, and therefore not his own work. They also acknowledge it is based on God's foreknowledge of who will be saved.

From John Calvin, the Reformer:

"Predestination we call the eternal decree of God, by which he has determined in himself the destiny of every man. For they are not all created in the same condition, but eternal life is foreordained for some, and eternal damnation for others. Every man, therefore, being created for one or the other of these ends, we say, he is predestinated either to life or to death."[16] After quoting Calvin, Dr. Enns comments: "The doctrine of predestination involves election to salvation and reprobation to eternal condemnation. Calvin emphasized the necessity of both. While election to salvation is entirely of God's grace, reprobation is just because it is due to sin and guilt."

Note: This view is called "***unconditional election***", the "U" in the TULIP acronym of the Five Points of Calvinist doctrine.

The "Arminian" view, as described by Alister E. McGrath:

"Arminius argued that predestination did not involve God's decision to determine which specific individuals would be saved, but rather which groups of people would be redeemed. God determined from all eternity that those who had faith would be saved. But it was up to the individual to come to faith."[17]

Note: Arminians teach that election is ***conditional upon man's cooperation with God,*** because he has the free will to "choose" God.

Comparative Views of Election

Lutheran	Arminian	Calvinist
Election is *conditional* on God's foreknowledge of a person's faith. (see further explanation in endnotes.)[18]	Election is *conditional* on God's foreknowledge of man's cooperation with God's grace.	Election is *unconditional:* based on God's will, or choice.

Sanctification: What now? How do I live as a believer?

When our daughter, Kari, was just a toddler, her father and I visited a clothing store in hopes of finding a suit (inexpensive, we hoped!) for her dad who was a newly-ordained pastor. Our young salesman had beautiful long hair, which was the style of the day. When he was out of earshot, Kari whispered to me, "Is he Jesus?" I knew Tim to be a believer and realized that he would be happy to be mistaken for Jesus, since that is the true desire of every Christian—to be like his Lord and Savior, his Master.

So how does that happen? Is it a process or an event? What part does our effort play in it? Theologians call this the doctrine of Sanctification.

God's solution for condemnation: justification
God's solution for contamination: sanctification
-John Piper, from sermon notes

This is most certainly true…

232. What is sanctification?
Sanctification is the gracious work of the Holy Spirit by which He daily renews me more and more in the image of God through the Word and Sacraments. (I Thessalonians 5:23,24; Philippians 2:12,13)

233. How does sanctification show itself in your daily life?
It is shown in a growing love for God and other people, a desire to do His will in all things, and also by self-denial in striving against the devil, the world and my own sinful human nature. (Ephesians 3:16-19; Colossians 2:6,7; Matthew 16:24)

234. Do you remain saved by your own good life?
No, my Lord Jesus Christ has done everything necessary for my justification and sanctification, and I can depend completely upon Him. (I Corinthians 1:30)

-Explanation of Luther's Small Catechism

"People do not drift toward holiness. Apart from grace-driven effort, people do not gravitate toward godliness, prayer, obedience to Scripture, faith, and delight in the Lord. We drift toward compromise and call it tolerance; we drift toward disobedience and call it freedom; we drift toward superstition and call it faith. We cherish the indiscipline of lost self-control and call it relaxation; we slouch toward prayerlessness and delude ourselves into thinking we have escaped legalism; we slide toward godlessness and convince ourselves we have been liberated."[19]

-D.A.Carson

You are now adopted into the family. God is truly your *Father*, Jesus is your *brother*, the Holy Spirit is your *helper*, and you have millions of believing *siblings in the Lord,* in this family—this household of faith. You are a "new creation" with a new nature: "*If anyone is in Christ, he is a new creation; the old has gone, the new has come*!" (2 Corinthains 5:17)

Works—or behavior—now is not to affirm your place in the family. God has already opened the door and adopted you, based entirely on His work of salvation. It is not even to confirm your place, to prove that you belong. Your good behavior now is motivated by love for your Father, a desire to "make Him look good" in the eyes of the

Written on the headstone of Ruth Bell Graham's grave, at her request:

"*End of construction. Thank you for your patience.*"

world (to "glorify Him", as the Bible states it). As a believer your desire is to please Him who gave His very life to save you. You want to "*abide in Him*" (John 15 uses the word picture of Jesus as the vine; we are the branches), allowing His Holy Spirit to live in and flow through you, causing growth in faith and in fruits of the Spirit. Paul, in Galatians 5 writes, "Live by the Spirit and you will not gratify the desires of the sinful nature," and he proceeds to list some truly terrible sins. But then he lists the fruits of the Spirit of God at work in the believer:

Love	Joy	Peace
Patience	Kindness	Goodness
Faithfulness	Gentleness	Self-control

Notice that these virtues are *produced by the life in the tree*—the Holy Spirit of God. They are not ornaments to be *placed on the tree*.

So, with this new nature inside, what is *NEW*?

> "Where there are no good works there is no faith. If works and love do not blossom forth, it is not genuine faith, the Gospel has not yet gained a foothold, and Christ is not yet rightly known."
> -Martin Luther
>
> "Christianity without discipleship is always Christianity without Christ."[20]
> -Dietrich Bonhoeffer
>
> "God does not need our good works, but our neighbor does."[21]
> -Gustav Wingren

- **A new Master:**

"This is love for God: to obey his commands. And his commands are not burdensome, for everyone born of God has overcome the world. This is the victory that has overcome the world, even our faith." (I John 5:3-5)

"Do you not know that your body is a temple of the Holy Spirit, who is in you, whom you have received from God? You are not your own; you were bought at a price. Therefore honor God with your body." (I Corinthians. 6:19-20)

"Teach me, O Lord, to follow your decrees; then I will keep them to the end . . . Direct me in the path of your commands, for there I find delight." (Psalm 119:33, 35)

- **A new sensitivity towards sin**

"For the grace of God that brings salvation has appeared to all men. It teaches us to say "No" to ungodliness and worldly passions, and to live self-controlled, upright and godly lives in this present age, while we wait for the blessed hope—the glorious appearing of our great God and Savior, Jesus Christ, who gave himself for us to redeem us from all wickedness and to purify for himself a people that are his very own, eager to do what is good." (Titus 2:11-13)

"Search me, O God, and know my heart; test me and know my anxious thoughts. See if there is any offensive way in me, and lead me in the way everlasting." (Psalm 139:23-24)

- **A new motivation to tell others**

"You are a chosen people, a royal priesthood, a holy nation, a people belonging to God, that you may declare the praises of him who called you out of darkness into his wonderful light." (I Peter 2:9)

"You will receive power when the Holy Spirit comes on you; and you will be my witnesses in Jerusalem, and in all Judea and Samaria, and to the ends of the earth." (Acts 1:8)

- **A new love for the Word**

"I have hidden your word in my heart that I might not sin against you . . . I rejoice in following your statutes as one rejoices in great riches. I meditate on your precepts and consider your ways. I delight in your decrees; I will not neglect your word . . . I delight in your commandments because I love them. (Psalm 119:11, 14-16, 47)

"(The blessed man's) delight is in the law of the Lord, and on his law he meditates day and night." (Psalm 1:2)

- **A new freedom from guilt of the past**

"Do you not know that the wicked will not inherit the kingdom of God? Do not be deceived: Neither the sexually immoral nor idolaters nor adulterers nor male prostitutes nor homosexual offenders nor thieves nor the greedy nor drunkards nor slanderers nor swindlers will inherit the kingdom of God. **And that is what some of you were.** [boldface, mine] BUT you were washed, you were sanctified, you were justified in the name of the Lord Jesus Christ and by the Spirit of our God." (I Corinthians. 6:9-11)

"If we walk in the light, as he is in the light, we have fellowship with one another, and the blood of Jesus, his Son, purifies us **from every sin**." [boldface, mine] (I John 1:7)

- **A new desire to pray**

"Have mercy on me, O Lord, for I call to you all day long. Bring joy to your servant, for to you, O Lord, I lift up my soul . . . Hear my prayer, O Lord; listen to my cry for mercy. In the day of my trouble I will call to you, for you will answer me." (Psalm. 86:3, 6-7)

- **A new assurance of eternal life**

"My sheep listen to my voice; I know them, and they follow me. I give them eternal life, and they shall never perish; no one can snatch them out of my hand." (John 10:27-28)

"I am not ashamed, because I know whom I have believed, and am convinced that he is able to guard what I have entrusted to him for that day." (2 Timothy 1:12)

- **A new battle, for I now have two natures, and they are in conflict:**

"We have this treasure in jars of clay to show that this all-surpassing power is from God and not from us. We are hard pressed on every side, but not crushed; perplexed, but not in despair; persecuted, but not abandoned; struck down, but not destroyed. We always carry around in our body the death of Jesus, so that the life of Jesus may also be revealed in our body." (2 Corinthians 4:7-10)

"I find this law at work: When I want to do good, evil is right there with me. For in my inner being I delight in God's law, but I see another law at work in the members of my body, waging war against the law of my mind and making me a prisoner of the law of sin at work within my members . . . Who will rescue me? . . . Thanks be to God—through Jesus Christ our Lord!" (Romans 7:21-25)

- **A new "fear" of God**

There is a new understanding of His holiness; a reverence, respect, and a desire not to offend Him. It is an intimate relationship of love, but it is not casual, for He is the holy, Almighty God. In the *Explanation to Luther's Small Catechism*, the meanings for each commandment begin, "We should fear and love God so that we . . ."

- **A new purpose**

Paul writes, "Since the day we heard about you, we have not stopped praying for you and asking God to fill you with the knowledge of his will through all spiritual wisdom and understanding. And we pray this in order that you may live a life worthy of the Lord and may please him in every way: bearing fruit in every good work, growing in the knowledge of God." (Colossians 1:9-10)

- **A new confidence**

"Since we have a great high priest...let us approach the throne of grace with confidence, so that we may receive mercy and find grace to help us in our time of need." (Heb. 4:14-16)

"Let us draw near to God with a sincere heart in full assurance of faith . . ." (Heb. 10:22)

- **A new peace**

With God: "Therefore, since we have been justified through faith, we have peace with God through our Lord Jesus Christ, through whom we have gained access by faith into this grace in which we now stand." (Romans 5:1)

In our hearts: "Do not be anxious about anything, but in everything, by prayer and petition, with thanksgiving, present your requests to God. And the peace of God, which transcends all understanding, will guard your hearts and your minds in Christ Jesus." (Philippians 4:6-7)

With others: "Live in harmony with one another; be sympathetic, love as brothers, be compassionate and humble. Do not repay evil with evil or insult with insult, but with blessing, because to this you were called . . ." (I Peter 3:8-9)

- **A new ability to serve God**

"Each one should use whatever gift he has received to serve others, faithfully administering God's grace in its various forms. If anyone speaks, he should do it as one speaking the very words of God. If anyone serves, he should do it with the strength God provides, so that in all things God may be praised through Jesus Christ . . ." (I Peter 4:10-11)

"Always give yourselves fully to the work of the Lord, because you know that your labor in the Lord is not in vain." (1 Corinthians 15:58)

- **A new testimony**

"I will sing of your strength, in the morning I will sing of your love; for you are my fortress, my refuge in times of trouble. O my Strength, I sing praise to you . . ." (Psalm 59:16)

- **A new gratitude**

"The Lord is my strength and my shield; my heart trusts in him, and I am helped. My heart leaps for joy and I will give thanks to him in song." (Psalm 28:7)

"I will extol the Lord at all times; his praise will always be on my lips...Glorify the Lord with me; let us exalt his name together. I sought the Lord, and he answered me; he delivered me from all my fears." (Psalm 34:1-4)

"Let them give thanks to the Lord for his unfailing love and his wonderful deeds for men, for he satisfies the thirsty and fills the hungry with good things." (Psalm 107:8)

Note: The reasons for gratitude to God could fill an entire bookcase of volumes!

- **A new comforter**

"He will call upon me, and I will answer him; I will be with him in trouble, I will deliver him and honor him." (Psalm 91:15)

"May our Lord Jesus Christ himself and God our Father, who loved us and by his grace gave us eternal encouragement and good hope, encourage your hearts and strengthen you in every good deed and word." (2 Thessalonians 2:16-17)

"Praise be to the God and Father of our Lord Jesus Christ, the Father of compassion and the God of all comfort, who comforts us in all our troubles, so that we can comfort those in any trouble with the comfort we ourselves have received from God." (2 Corinthians 3-4)

- **A new companion**

"God has said, 'Never will I leave you; never will I forsake you.' So we say with confidence, 'The Lord is my helper; I will not be afraid. What can man do to me?'" (Hebrews 13:5b-6), and "Jesus Christ is the same yesterday and today and forever." (vs. 8)

"Be strong and courageous. Do not be terrified; do not be discouraged, for the Lord your God will be with you wherever you go." (Joshua 1:9)

- **A new employer**

"Whatever you do, work at it with all your heart, as working for the Lord, not for men since you know that you will receive an inheritance from the Lord as a reward. It is the Lord Christ you are serving." (Colossians 3:23-24)

"Teach me to do your will, for you are my God." (Psalm 143:10)

- **A new love**

"Though you have not seen him, you love him; and even though you do not see him now, you believe in him and are filled with an inexpressible and glorious joy, for you are receiving the goal of your faith, the salvation of your souls." (I Peter 1:8-9)

"We love because he first loved us." (I John 4:19).

- **A new security**

"The eternal God is our refuge, and underneath are the everlasting arms." (Deut. 33:27)

"He who dwells in the shelter of the Most High will rest in the shadow of the Almighty. I will say of the Lord, 'He is my refuge and my fortress, my God, in whom I trust.'" (Ps. 91:1,2)

- **A new hope/destination**

"Our citizenship is in heaven. And we eagerly await a Savior from there, the Lord Jesus Christ, who, by the power that enables him to bring everything under his control, will transform our lowly bodies so that they will be like his glorious body." (Philippians 3:20-21)

"Now there is in store for me the crown of righteousness, which the Lord, the righteous Judge, will award to me on that day—and not only to me, but also to all who have longed for his appearing." (2 Timothy 4:8-9)

- **A new defender: My enemies include the world, the devil, and my own nature.**

"You have been a refuge for the poor, a refuge for the needy in his distress, a shelter from the storm and a shade from the heat." (Isaiah 25:4)

"The Lord is my light and my salvation—whom shall I fear? The Lord is the stronghold of my life—of whom shall I be afraid?" (Psalm 27:1)

- **A new Guide**

"You guide me with your counsel, and afterward you will take me into glory." (Psalm73:24)

"I will instruct you and teach you in the way you should go; I will counsel you and watch over you." (Psalm 32:8)

- **A new provision**

"God is able to make all grace abound to you, so that in all things at all times, having all that you need, you will abound in every good work." (2 Corinthians 9:8)

"My God will meet all your needs according to his glorious riches in Christ Jesus." (Philippians 4:19)

"Do not worry, saying, 'What shall we eat?' or 'What shall we drink," or 'What shall we wear?'. . . But seek first his kingdom and his righteousness, and all these things will be given to you as well." (Matthew 6:31-33)

- **A new heart**

"I will give you a new heart and put a new spirit in you; I will remove from you your heart of stone and give you a heart of flesh. And I will put my Spirit in you and move you to follow my decrees and be careful to keep my laws . . ." (Ezekiel 33:26-27)

And it is all by grace! "It is because of him that you are in Christ Jesus, who has become for us wisdom from God—that is, our righteousness, holiness and redemption. Therefore, as it is written: 'Let him who boasts boast in the Lord.' " (I Corinthians 1:30-31)

A part of this new life is the reality that it will result in a **new "call to suffer**" because the believer now walks the narrow road (Matthew 7:13) and there is opposition on every side

But God has promised to walk beside His children and to bring them safely home!

So, what else is new?

Maybe you should write your own list, tape it to your mirror and use it to inspire daily praise to your God! Remember, "It is good to praise the Lord and make music to your name, O Most High, to proclaim your love in the morning and your faithfulness at night . . . " (Psalm 92:1-2)

John Wesley's Rule:

Do all the good you can
By all the means you can
In all the ways you can
In all the places you can
At all the times you can
To all the people you can,
As long as ever you can. [22]

"The nub of the matter is this. Salvation is completely God's work; but a saved person is a changed person. He or she has a new nature, a new life, new desires." [23]
-Dr. Dale Varberg

Comparative Views of Sanctification

What is agreed among most Protestant churches:

Stanley N. Gundry states in the introduction to his book, *Five Views on Sanctification:* "First, all agree that the Bible teaches a sanctification that is past, present, and future. It is past because it begins in a position of separation already gained in Christ's completed work. It is present in that it describes a process of cultivating a holy life. And sanctification has a future culmination at the return of Christ, when the effects of sin will be fully removed. Second, all agree that the process of sanctification requires believers to strive to express God's love in their experience. They must devote themselves to the traditional Christian disciplines and daily make the hard choices against evil and for God's ways of righteousness. Finally, all agree that the Bible promises success in this process of struggling against personal sin, through the power of the Holy Spirit." [24]

Lutheran	Arminian	Calvinist
Sanctification is a *process*; one grows in Christ-likeness in faithful obedience to the Word and through the work of God's Spirit in the believer. Perfection is not achieved until heaven.	Entire sanctification is a work of the Spirit subsequent to the new birth by which fully consecrated believers are cleansed of all sin. Sometimes called "sinless perfection." It is *an event* rather than process. Sin is understood as being *intentional* transgression.	Similar to the Lutheran view. Sanctification is a life-long *process.* Like Lutherans, sin is viewed as transgression against God's law; it may be "commission" (intentionally committing sin) or "omission" (failing to do good).

Legalism, Lordship, and License

When speaking of sanctification—the growth in Christian virtue—the subject of "legalism" always arises. Conscientious believers are sometimes seen as living by a long list of "do's and don'ts" and condemning of others whose lists don't match their own. This is a huge topic and fraught with misunderstanding and accusation. It cannot be ignored but can only be addressed briefly here. Many resources for further study are included in the bibliography.

Three uses of God's Law:

- The political use of the law

This enables people to *live together in community*. It awards good behavior and punishes bad behavior and is necessary for the orderly functioning of societies. Governments, parents, and teachers all use the law in this way. It "**curbs** and regulates the horizontal realm."

- The theological use of the Law

This is the "**mirror**" that *shows us our sinfulness*, our broken relationship with a holy God. Luther called this the Law's primary function because it was vital that we recognize our sinfulness, and are then driven to Christ to save us from our sins. (See Romans 7). It deals with our "vertical" relationship, our relationship to God.

- The instructive use of the Law

This teaches us moral behavior, how a believer should conduct himself. "The Law functions to keep us in line and to accuse and condemn us whether we believe in Christ or not. But as believers encounter God's Law in daily life, they not only encounter it as an enticing or threatening curb and as an accusing and condemning mirror. We also turn to the Law for information regarding decisions we have to make as Christians. We need that information because our minds are not totally transformed into properly functioning human minds at conversion any more than our wills are transformed into absolutely trusting wills."[25]

- Robert Kolb in *The Christian Faith*

Legalism, according to Professor Omar Gjerness, is the attempt to force man to correct moral behavior with the use of law. It is a force from *outside* the individual. Morality, rather, is ethics from *within.* There are two extremes in relation to the law: **legalism** (coercion by law, which can result in arbitrary lists of approved and disapproved behavior), or **license** (the view that believers can live without the law; lawlessness—an antinomian heresy which we reject). On one hand, Christianity can be reduced to compliance with a list of rules, or on the other hand, in reaction, Christians can abuse their freedom in Christ, becoming careless and tolerant of sin. So how is this dilemma solved? Gjerness writes, "The solution of the dilemma caused by the tension between legalism and license does not lie in a compromise between extremes. . . It is an entirely new answer." This answer is the Lordship of Jesus Christ. "After a person yields his heart to Christ, becomes a Christian, and accepts the Lordship of Jesus Christ, there is a sense in which he no longer has any relationship to the law. He is not under its condemnation, nor under its jurisdiction. However, the law

John 14:15: "If you love me, you will keep my commandments."
-Jesus

Micah 6:6-8: "He has showed you, O man, what is good. And what does the Lord require of You? To act justly and to love mercy and to walk humbly with your God."

still has a teaching function to a Christian. A Christian may determine whether an act is moral or immoral through the study of the Scriptures."[26]

The good behavior of a believer, then, is *motivated internally*, by the presence of Jesus in His life, and by his desire to please his Lord. His actions may be similar to those of legalists, but his motivation is entirely different, as Dr. Francis Schaeffer observed in his excellent book, *True Spirituality* (see bibliography). For further reading on the doctrine of sanctification see *Five Views on Sanctification*, Stanley Gundry, editor.

> *"If I please Jesus, it doesn't matter who I displease; if I displease Jesus it doesn't matter who I please."*
> -Adrian Rogers[27]

Eternal Security, also called Preservation of the Saints:
Can a person fall away from faith?

In my college years I had a godly professor whom I greatly respected who asserted that once a person was saved, he would never be lost. The word picture he used described faith as a house: a person may "fall down" in the house, but not "fall out" of it. But I realized that—sadly—that person could choose to walk out of the house; he was not a prisoner. Also, sadly, I have observed such falling away among friends who once professed and demonstrated living, active belief in Christ as Savior, but who have now denied Him. They did not so much "lose" their faith, as "leave" their faith.

> "The perseverance of the saints means that all those who are truly born again will be kept by God's power and will persevere as Christians until the end of their lives, and that only those who persevere until the end have been truly born again"[28]
> - Dr. Wayne Grudem

This issue of the secure destiny of a believer in Jesus is one which has divided sincere Christians for centuries. There are essentially two views, with some shades of differences within each view. In the Calvinist system of theology, the "P" in the TULIP acronym represents "preservation of the saints." They believe that the Scriptures teach that once a person is truly saved he will never fall away from his faith—he will never be eternally lost. Some acknowledge that he may *backslide or stray,* but never completely abandon faith. They cite Scripture such as John 10:28, "I give them eternal life, and they shall never perish; no one can snatch them out of my hand," and John 3:36, "He who believes in the Son has eternal life."

Others respond that, although a saved person possesses the life of Christ which is eternal, he does not necessarily eternally possess that life; he can abandon it, in the same way that he received it. If that were not so, he would have no free will. They refer to Scriptures which warn of unbelief and appear to make security conditional on continuing in obedience and faith. "Now he has reconciled you by Christ's physical body through death to present you holy in his sight, without blemish and free from accusation—if you continue in your faith, established and firm, not moved from the hope held out in the gospel." (Colossians 1:22-23) A similar passage in Hebrews 3:14 states, "We have come to share in Christ if we hold firmly till the end the confidence we had at first." They also cite Hebrews 6:1-6 where Paul declares, "It is impossible for those who have once been enlightened, who have tasted the heavenly gift, who have shared in the Holy Spirit, who have tasted the goodness of the word of God and the powers of the coming age, if they fall away, to be brought back to repentance, because to their loss they are crucifying the Son of God all over again and subjecting him to public disgrace." Dr. Irwin Lutzer and other theologians will respond either that these were not really believers in the first place, or that they are not really "falling away" into damnation but to loss of blessing. [29] Dr. Charles Ryrie, in attempting to explain this passage writes in the notes of his study Bible, "Others understand the passage to be a warning to genuine believers to urge them on in Christian growth and maturity. To 'fall away' is impossible (since, according to this view, true believers are eternally secure), but the phrase is placed in the sentence to strengthen the warning. It is similar to saying something like this to a class of students: 'It is impossible for a student, once enrolled in this course, if he turns the clock back (which cannot be done), to start the course over. Therefore, let all students go on to deeper knowledge.'" [30] To Arminians and Lutherans, this seems a convoluted position.

Lutherans do not believe in the doctrine of eternal security, or "preservation of the saints." We believe it is possible for a child born into the kingdom of God by baptism to apostatize (to abandon his faith). If the nature of sin is rebellion and unbelief, then a child's mind and will must be brought into subjection to God when these become active. Such subjection is necessary for everyone. If a baptized person yields his or her life to God he continues in faith. If he does not do so, he departs from the faith.

A common misunderstanding among some who believe in the doctrine of eternal security is that Lutherans teach that believers "jump in and out of salvation" in a cycle of sin/repentance/confession/forgiveness—and then sin again. There would then be no assurance of salvation, no comfort in the gospel! There would be daily fear that a particular sin was unconfessed and therefore salvation was lost. That is a total misrepresentation of the Lutheran view. The specific point at which a person is hardened by *persistent sin and unbelief* (the definition of apostasy) is unknown to us, but since Scripture is filled with dire warning about it (particularly in Hebrews) we know it can occur, or those warnings would be unnecessary. We would assert that there is less assurance of salvation in the Calvinist view, since those who teach this doctrine contend that if one appears to deny or desert his faith it is proof that he never was truly saved.

Comparison of Views of Eternal Security

Lutheran	Arminian	Calvinist
Believers can be lost if they fall away or turn from faith	Believers can be lost if they fall away or turn from faith	The elect will never be lost; they are eternally secure
The remedy is repentance and conversion	The remedy is repentance and conversion	"Backsliding" is possible, but is evidence that the person's salvation was not genuine.

"*Of Repentance they teach that for those who have fallen after Baptism there is a remission of sins whenever they are converted; and that the church ought to impart absolution to those thus returning to repentance…*" -Concordia Triglotta, p. 49, Article 12 of the Augsburg Confession

For further reading: *4 Views on Eternal Security*, Stan N. Gundry, editor. This is an excellent resource since each position is presented by one who holds that conviction, and each position is responded to by the others. See also a large section in Wayne Grudem's *Systematic Theology*; *The Doctrines that Divide* by Erwin Lutzer; *The Christian Faith* by Robert Kolb; *Moody Handbook of Theology*, Paul Enns (see bibliography)

Endnotes:

---

1. C. S. Lewis, *Mere Christianity* (New York: Harper Collins, 1952, 2001), 56.
2. Omar Gjerness, *Knowing Good from Evil: A Study in Ethics* (Fergus Falls, MN: Faith & Fellowship Publishing, 1985), 41.
3. Ibid., 42-43.
4. Martin Luther, *The Babylonian Captivity of the Church*, quoted in Alister E. McGrath, gen. ed., *Zondervan Handbook of Christian Beliefs* (Grand Rapids:Zondervan, 2005), 314.
5. Steven Heppner, from personal correspondence with the author. Used by permission.
6. Gjerness, *Knowing Good from Evil,* 59.
7. McGrath, *Zondervan Handbook of Christian Beliefs*, 329.
8. Ibid., 339.
9. Keith and Kristyn Getty, "Beneath the Cross", c. 2006 ThankYou Music.
10. Korey Maas, *Justification and Sanctification* (St. Louis: Concordia Publishing House, 2005), 25.
11. George W. Chadwick, "I Sought the Lord, and Afterward I Knew", in *Hymns* (Chicago: InterVarsity Christian Fellowship, 1952), 78.
12. Roger Olson, "Election is for Everyone", *Christianity Today* (January/February, 2013), 42.
13. Peter Kreeft, *Handbook of Christian Apologetics* (Downers Grove, IL: InterVarsity Press, 1994), 384-385.
14. M. E. Sletta, quoted by Dale Varberg, *Faith and Fellowship: A Look at Lutheran Brethren Theology 1900-2000* (Fergus Falls, MN: Faith & Fellowship Publishing, 2000), 93-96
15. Robert Kolb, The Christian Faith (St. Louis: Concordia Publishing, 1993), 176.
16. Paul Enns, *The Moody Handbook of Theology* (Chicago: Moody Publishers, 2008), 477.
17. McGrath, *Zondervan Handbook of Christian Beliefs*, 207.
18. Robert M. Overgaard, Sr., former President of the Church of the Lutheran Brethren, in personal correspondence to the author explains election this way, "I believe the term 'in Christ Jesus' occurs 139 times in the New Testament. In Paul's writing it becomes a technical term about a relationship with God that is by grace through faith in Christ Jesus. With that in mind, read all references to election in Ephesians. Conclusion: We are elected 'in Christ Jesus' to be saved. Therefore, since this means of salvation was chosen by God before the foundations of the earth were laid, this is the basis of election. God elects all who trust in Christ Jesus to salvation and to works that are prepared for them to walk in. Therefore we say to all, 'Whosoever will may come. Come to Christ; God elected to save all who trust Him.' Election is comforting because it is an election to give salvation to any and all who trust in what God has done in Christ Jesus. The door is chosen and the invitation is given. To those who respond to God's call in faith, He exercises His Lordship to predestine their lives as He will. They agree because He is Lord." Used by permission.
19. D. A. Carson, *For the Love of God* (Wheaton, IL: Crossway, 2006).
20. Dietrich Bonhoeffer, *The Cost of Discipleship* (New York: Touchstone, 1937, 1995), 59.
21. Gustav Wingren, "Luther on Vocation", trans. Carl C. Rasmussen (Evansville, IN: Ballast, 1994), 10.
22. "Rule of Conduct", in George Eayrs, ed. *Letters of John Wesley*, 1915.
23. Varberg, *Faith and Fellowship*, 177.

24. Stanley N. Gundry, series ed., *Five Views on Sanctification* (Grand Rapids: Zondervan, 1987), 7.
25. Robert Kolb, *The Christian Faith* (St. Louis: Concordia Publishing, 1993), 118.
26. Gjerness, *Knowing Good From Evil*, 27.
27. Adrian Rogers, from his message," Why is Faith Important?", Love Worth Finding Ministries. Online at www.lwf.org.
28. Wayne Grudem, *Systematic Theology, An Introduction to Biblical Doctrine* (Grand Rapids: Zondervan, 1994), 788.
29. Irwin Lutzer, *The Doctrines That Divide* (Grand Rapids: Kregel Publications, 1998), 228.
30. Charles Ryrie, *The Ryrie Study Bible*—New American Standard translation (Chicago: Moody Press, 1978), 1843.

Chapter 6

The Sacraments: God's Means of Grace to Sinners

The Sacraments: God's Means of Grace to Sinners

He was just a small boy, "young enough to crawl beneath the pews. Short enough to stand up on the seats of pews when the congregation arose to sing hymns, and still be hidden...old enough to want to see Jesus. Young enough to believe that the mortal eye could ***see Jesus."*** *And oh, how he wanted to see Him! After an exhausting, secretive, and futile search of his church, that child ultimately found Him in his mother, as she returned to her seat from receiving the Lord's Supper. In an account that brought me to tears, Walter Wangerin, Jr. tells of his discovery: ". . . Jesus! She told me where Jesus was at! Not far away from me at all. Closer to me than I ever thought possible. In my mama! He never had been hiding. I'd been looking wrong. My mighty mother was his holy temple all along." He shocked her by throwing his little arms around her neck, with the sheer joy of discovering the Gospel.* [1]

Christian churches use various terms and have various understandings about several observances which Christ instituted for His believing church. Whatever the differences in views, these observances have deep meaning for Christians and ought to be observed with joy and gratitude to the One whose grace comes to us without any goodness on our part.

"Means of Grace"

Lutherans believe that God's grace comes to us through "means", or vehicles which convey it. We believe that there are three: **the Word of God, Baptism, and the Lord's Supper**. The term used for this doctrine is "*mediate grace*" i.e., God uses means. That is not to say that He may not bring His grace to us in other ways, but we do know that He does use these.

This is most certainly true….

331. What is a sacrament?

A sacrament is a holy act, instituted by Christ, in which by visible means, He gives and confirms His invisible grace.

332. What are the sacraments of the New Testament?

The sacraments of the New Testament are Baptism and the Lord's Supper.

333. What were the rites of the Old Testament which foreshadowed the sacrments of the New Testament?

The rites of the Old Testament which foreshadowed the sacraments of the new Testament were Circumcision and the Passover meal.

- Explanation of Luther's Small Catechism

Ordinance or Sacrament

Those (including Lutherans) who believe in the "*means of grace*" usually refer to these observances as "*sacraments*", which Augustine described as "the visible form of an invisible grace". The term comes from the Latin *sacramentum,* which means "a thing set apart as sacred." The word conveys the idea of mystery, something impossible for us to fully grasp but which we believe Scripture clearly teaches. Other Protestants use the term "*ordinances*" which removes the idea of "*means of grace*,' and rather sees them as "*rites*" prescribed by Christ.

Number of Sacraments

Roman Catholics recognize *seven sacraments*: baptism, the Eucharist (Lord's Supper), confirmation, penance, extreme unction (last rites), holy orders (ordination of clergy), and marriage.

- Protestants historically recognize only *two*: baptism and the Lord's Supper, as these were the only observances directly instituted by Christ.

Sacrament of The Lord's Supper

Terms:

- **Eucharist**—used primarily by Roman Catholics and Orthodox. Comes from the Greek term meaning "the giving of thanks."
- **Holy Communion**. Conveys the idea of our holy God "communing" with us in the supper, and also the communing with fellow believers.
- **Lord's Supper**. The reference to the Passover Meal, the occasion at which Christ instituted it.
- Sometimes also "**the sacrament of the altar**."

The Communion service

In the Lutheran church, the service normally includes these elements, whether in liturgy spoken by the congregants or by the pastor alone. It is important that the Word be included, as a sacrament is not only the visible means (bread and wine), but is connected to the Word.

1. A re-telling of Christ's death .(Luke 23:33-43; Matthew 27:45-46; John 19:28-30)

2. The words of invitation and promise of forgiveness. (I John 1:9; Matthew 11:28; John 3:16,17)

3. A time of silent personal confession, reflection, meditation and prayer.

4. The verbal confession of the Christian faith, stated in the Apostles' Creed.

5. The words of institution. (I Corinthians 11:23-24; Matthew 26:27-28; I Corinthians 11:25; I Corinthians 10:16-17). These passages include the important words of Christ: "This is my body, which is for you; do this in remembrance of me." and, "This is my blood of the covenant, which is poured out for many for the forgiveness of sins . . . Do this, whenever you drink it, in remembrance of me."

Agreements among Protestant churches

Despite differing views on the meaning of this meal, Christians are agreed that,

- It should be observed; it should not be neglected.
- The taking of communion does not guarantee that one is a true believer.
- The meal is important and should be viewed seriously and reverently, preceded by an examination of oneself. We are warned that disregarding it is to disregard Christ Himself. (II Cor. 11:27-30)
- This meal is to be observed frequently. Many churches observe it weekly, while others do so monthly.

> "We affirm that the main thing in a sacrament is the Word and the promise of Christ. Without the Word, there is nothing there. The validity of the sacrament does not come from the officiant, the faith of the participant, or the right procedures. Its validity comes from the completed work of Christ on the cross and the fact that God has instituted it. The sacraments are not different ways of salvation; they are different ways of delivering what Christ has done for the salvation of humankind. In the preached Word we hear of Christ with our ears, in the sacramental Word we hear of Christ with our touch and taste and smell and sight. We must be clear on this; the sacraments deliver the person and the work of Christ. They are ways of preaching the Gospel. They are visual promises from God to us in Christ." [2]
>
> \- Tim Ysteboe

Disagreements among Christian churches

Disagreements are primarily about the meaning or benefits and the state of the elements. Roman Catholics and Lutherans view forgiveness as a benefit, while the other two do not.

1. **Roman Catholic view**, known as "*transubstantiation*". The elements of bread and wine, when consecrated, are understood to actually become the body and blood of Christ, though their physical appearance does not change.
2. **The Lutheran view**, sometimes called "*consubstantiation*" by non-Lutherans, but more accurately the "*Real Presence*," understands the body and blood of the Lord being "in, under, and between" the physical elements of bread and wine. They are more than symbols, since Christ carefully stated, "This IS my body...This IS my blood." The illustration is sometimes given of a sponge which may contain water, though it remains a sponge. Luther used the idea of iron, which may contain heat, but does not become heat. It is undeniably a mystery, but we honor a God who is far above our understanding. "Consubstantiation" would mean "alongside", rather than "within", and is viewed as a less-accurate term.
3. **The Calvinist view** stresses the mystical, spiritual connection between Christ and the physical elements but believes that He is *spiritually but not physically* present in them. Calvinists acknowledge that it is more than mere "memorial", or else it would not be accompanied by such dire warnings of misuse and disregard.
4. **The Memorial/Commemorative view**, held by many other Protestants, understands the elements as being *representative symbols* of Christ's body and blood. He is not physically or substantially present in them. The service is seen as a memorial, remembering the sacrifice of Christ for us.

This is most certainly true…

368. What do you receive when you take part in the Lord's Supper?

In, with and under the bread and wine, I receive the body and blood of Jesus Christ which He gave for me.

370. What makes the bread and wine a sacrament?

God's own word, which is connected to the bread and wine, makes it a sacrament.

372. For whom is the Lord's Supper intended?

The Lord's Supper is intended only for believers in Jesus who are old enough to be taught and who can examine themselves. (I Corinthians 11:27-29)

373. What benefits do you as a believer receive from the Lord's Supper?

When I worthily receive the Lord's Supper, I receive forgiveness of sin; I enter into a closer fellowship with Christ my Savior, and I am strengthened in faith, hope and love. (Matthew 26:27, 28)

374. How can physical eating and drinking produce such great benefits for you?

It is not the physical eating and drinking which bring great benefits but Jesus' own words of promise and assurance.

376. How would I receive the Lord's Supper unworthily?

I receive it unworthily when I do not believe the words spoken by Jesus, when I am not willing to forgive those who have sinned against me, and when I receive the Lord's Supper only out of habit.

379. Should you stay away from the Lord's Supper if you feel unworthy?

No, a sense of unworthiness is proper if it leads me to reach out for the worthiness of Jesus. (Matthew 5:3,6)

380. What should your attitude be as you eat the bread and drink the wine?

My attitude should be one of grateful remembrance for the suffering and death of Jesus on the cross for me and for the grace given to me in the bread and wine. (Luke 22:19c)

381. How should receiving Holy Communion affect your way of living?

Since I have received a holy gift from God in the Lord's Supper, I should live a holy life through the strength that Jesus gives. Philippians 1:27a; I Peter 2:24; Philippians 4:13)

- Explanation of Luther's Small Catechism

Comparative Views of the Lord's Supper

Roman Catholic	Lutheran	Arminian	Calvinist
It is a means of grace.	It is a means of grace.	It is a symbolic/ memorial only.	It is symbolic, but more than mere memorial.
The bread and wine are changed into Jesus' body and blood. (transubstantiation)	The bread and the wine remain truly bread and wine but Christ's body and blood are "in, under, and between" them. (the "Real Presence")	The bread and wine are only symbolic and are unchanged. (Baptist) Jesus is really present and his body and blood are spiritually present in the Lord's Supper. (Methodist)	Christ's body and blood are "spiritually present" in the elements of bread and wine.

Valuing the Meaning of the Lord's Supper

Alister McGrath, in the *Zondervan Handbook of Christian Beliefs*, cites three directions in which Christians may be said to look in the Lord's Supper:

- ***Back*** to the death of Christ, remembering that His sacrifice has atoned for our sins, once and for all.
- ***Forward***, to Christ's return and the great "marriage supper of the Lamb" which will someday occur. (Revelation 19:9)
- ***Around***, because of the shared experience of communion with one another, accompanied by love and unity. [3]

So, my fellow believer in Jesus, let us come with joy to His table, and join in the praise expressed in the ancient hymn of Johann Rist (1651 A.D.) from the *Concordia Hymnal:*

O living Bread from heaven, how hast Thou fed Thy guest!
The gifts Thou now hast given have filled my heart with rest.
O wondrous food of blessing, O cup that heals our woes!
My heart this gift possessing, in thankful song o'erflows.

Lord, grant me that, thus strengthened with heavenly food, while here
My course on earth is lengthened, I serve with holy fear.
And when Thou callest my spirit to leave this world below,
I enter through Thy merit, where joys unmingled flow. [4]

For further reading and study: *Understanding Four Views on the Lord's Supper*, Paul E. Engle, ed. This book includes direct quotes from Luther, Calvin, Wesley, Spurgeon and several church fathers, 19th and 20th century theologians, all the major faith confessions' statements regarding the Lord's Supper, as well as four pages of additional resources. See also *The Christian Faith* by Robert Kolb for a Lutheran view, and Wayne Grudem in *Systematic Theology* for the Calvinist view.

The Sacrament of Baptism

Baptism is the new beginning of a new belonging, and a new behaving.[5] - Alistair McGrath, Oxford University, UK

Jesus' words of institution in the Great Commission

"... All authority in heaven and on earth has been given to me. Therefore go and make disciples of all nations, baptizing them in the name of the Father and of the Son and of the Holy Spirit, and teaching them to obey everything I have commanded you. And surely I will be with you always, to the very end of the age." *(Matthew 28:18-19)*

The second of the two sacraments observed by the Protestant church is the sacrament of Baptism. As with the Lord's Supper, it is greatly valued because it was specifically instituted by Jesus Christ, and there are many areas of agreement in the way it is understood. There are also significant differences in view. As we study the issue, let us begin with humility, because much of God's plan is mystery to us, and godly men and women who love and observe the Scriptures may interpret them differently than we do. John H. Armstrong in his introduction to *Understanding Four Views on Baptism*, says it well:

"Let's be clear at the outset. There are godly, faithful and earnest students of the Bible who hold to different views about water baptism. Disagreement about baptism is not proof of rebellion, stupidity, or immaturity. Some of the most wonderful Christians you and I know fail to agree with one another about baptism."[6]

Agreements among most Protestant churches

- Baptism is central to the Christian faith.
- It is a commandment of Christ, not an option to carelessly observe.
- It is something God does, not something we do.
- It is a way for people to publicly show their commitment to God.
- It unites Christians as members of the body of Christ, the Church.
- It cannot be separated from faith in Christ Jesus. Salvation is through faith alone, in Christ alone. (Galatians 3:26-28; Ephesians 2:8-9)
- Not all who are baptized are truly and eternally saved.
- Baptism is not "magic." There is no benefit of the water apart from the Word and promise of God.
- Most would believe that baptism is to be administered once; while the Lord's Supper is to be observed often.
- Baptism is to be performed in the Name of the Triune God: Father, Son and Holy Spirit.

"...To be baptized in God's name is to be baptized not by men but by God himself. Although it is performed by men's hands, it is nevertheless truly God's act... The Word and the water must by no means be separated from each other. For where the Word is separated from the water, the water is no different from that which the maid cooks with and could indeed be called a bathkeeper's baptism. But when the Word is present according to God's ordinance, baptism is a sacrament, and it is called Christ's baptism...
Since we have learned the great benefit and power of baptism, let us observe further who receives these gifts and benefits of baptism. This again is most beautifully and clearly expressed in these same words, "He who believes and is baptized shall be saved," that is, faith alone makes the person worthy to receive the salutary divine water profitably...
Thus you plainly see that baptism is not a work which we do but is a treasure which God gives and faith grasps, just as the Lord Christ upon the cross is not a work but a treasure comprehended and offered to us in the Word and received by faith."[7]

- Martin Luther

Disagreements among Protestant churches

The areas of disagreement between Protestants all center around three major questions:

1. What does baptism **mean**?
2. What should be the **method** of baptism?
3. Who should **receive** baptism?

The views about method and recipients of baptism all flow from the understanding of the *meaning of baptism*.

Meaning— Three Views: *Initiation, Identification, or Infusion*

- ***Initiation.*** Baptism is understood as something that God does. It is a sacrament—a means of grace—through which a person is initiated into the family of God. It is often understood as a New Testament parallel to Old Testament circumcision. (I Corinthians 12:13) Lutherans and many others believe that regeneration takes place ("baptismal regeneration"). Presbyterians and Reformed see baptism as a "sign and seal" of salvation.
- ***Identification.*** Baptism is an act of profession of faith following repentance and conversion—a symbol of salvation. The believer is identifying with Christ in His death and resurrection and identifying himself as a believer in Jesus. Since a conscious understanding and verbalization of repentance and faith is considered necessary, baptism is for adults only. (Colossians 2:12)
- ***Infusion.*** Baptism is seen as "infusing" the believer with the power of the Holy Spirit. (Acts. 1:8) This view has appeared off and on throughout history, but has been seen most recently among the Pentecostals. Some Pentecostals, however, see this empowering as a "second blessing" rather than associated with water baptism. Most other Protestant churches believe that the Holy Spirit is given to the believer at water baptism or conversion.

Method– Three Views: *Pouring, Sprinkling, Immersion*

- ***Pouring***, also called "*affusion*". In this method, water was poured three times over the head of the one baptized, once for each member of the Trinity. It is understood to illustrate the pouring out of the Holy Spirit, as written in Acts 2:17-18. It seems most likely to have been used in the household baptisms of Cornelius (Acts 10:48) and the Philippian jailer (Acts 16:33), and it was also practiced in the early church as written in the *Didache* (early second century): "But concerning baptism, thus shall ye baptize. Having first recited all these things, baptize in the name of the Father and of the Son and of the Holy Spirit in living (running) water. But if thou has not living water, then baptize in other water; and if thou art not able in cold, then in warm. But if thou hast neither, then pour water on the head thrice in the name of the Father and of the Son and of the Holy Spirit."[8]
- ***Sprinkling***, also called "*aspersion*". The precedents of the ritual sprinkling for cleansing of the Levites (Number 8:5-7; 19:8-13) is referred to in Hebrews 9:10 as "baptism." Also in the third century Cyprian stated that the amount of water in baptism was not a significant factor in its importance. Those who adhere to this method also believe it more likely to have been the method used following the 3,000 conversions at Pentecost, when the lateness of the day and the distance from a large body of water would have made immersion less likely.

- ***Immersion.*** The person to be baptized is totally submerged in the water. This is to symbolize his identification with the death and resurrection of Jesus. Those who adhere to this method also reference Jesus' baptism "in the Jordan" and that He came up "out of the water." (Mark 1:9-10, Acts 8:38) They also cite the definition of baptize, which can mean "to immerse." For a full discussion of that definition, see *Modes and Meaning of Baptism* by Rev. Benjamin J. Johnson, a pastor in the Evangelical Free Church of America. (bibliography)

Recipients of Baptism

- ***Infant Baptism.*** Baptism is understood as something God Himself does, rather than something a person does in response to God. The faith that is necessary is a gift of God. They reference the covenant promise of God in Genesis 17:7 where children were included, and also the household baptism of the Philippian jailor (Acts 16:32-33) and Peter's statement in Acts 2:38-39, "Repent and be baptized, every one of you, in the name of Jesus Christ for the forgiveness of your sins. And you will receive the gift of the Holy Spirit. The promise is for you and your children and for all who are far off—for all whom the Lord our God will call." Infant baptism was practiced in the very early church, as seen in the writings of Origen (185-254 A.D.); Ireneus (a student of Polycarp, who was a student of the Apostle John), and Justin Martyr (martyred in 165 A.D.). [9]
- ***Believers' Baptism.*** Baptism is understood as a human response to God's grace and a public testimony of faith. Adherents refer to Scriptures which indicate repentance as a prerequisite for baptism, such as Acts 2:38, Acts 2:41, "Those who accepted his message were baptized…" and Acts 8:12, "But when they believed Philip as he preached the good news of the kingdom of God and the name of Jesus Christ, they were baptized, both men and women."

This is most certainly true…

341. Why should little children be baptized?

1. They are helpless and therefore the ideal people for salvation. (Luke 18:15-17)
2. They are sinners and need the grace of God. (Psalm 51:5)
3. They are capable of receiving the blessings of baptism. (Mark 10:15, 16)
4. They are capable of believing. (Matthew 18:6)
5. They are included in Jesus' command to "go into all nations." (Matthew 28:19, 20a; Acts 2:39)
6. They were included in the Old Testament and therefore would not be excluded in the New Testament unless plainly forbidden. (Colossians 2:11, 12)
7. The early church sets the example by baptizing entire households, which certainly must have included little children. (Acts 16:15, 33; I Corinthians 1:16)

-Explanation of Luther's Small Catechism

O Lord, Our Little Ones to Thee (*hymn by William Whiting, 1872*) [10]

O Lord, our little ones to Thee in faith and hope we give;
We know that through the mystery, their new-born souls shall live.
We pour the water on their brow, the sacred words we say;
Baptize them with the Spirit now, and keep them Thine alway.
Help them to go from strength to strength until, full-grown in Thee
They come before Thy face at length, and all Thy glory see.
And then, with all the heavenly host in everlasting songs,
Praise Father, Son, and Holy Ghost to whom all praise belongs.

Comparative Views of Baptism

	Lutheran	Baptist	Reformed/Calvinist
Meaning	It is a means of saving grace (baptismal regeneration). It is something God does for us by His grace. *Initiation*	It is a symbol of salvation, an outward sign of an inward change. It is done as a testimony of repentance. *Identification*	It is a "sign and seal" of the covenant. It is both the means of *initiation* into the covenant and a *sign* of salvation.
Method	May use any of the three; sprinkling or pouring is used with infants.	Immersion only.	May use any method, but sprinkling or pouring is used with infants.
Recipients	Infants, children and adults. Infants are capable of faith, through God's grace. Faith is actual, not potential. Adults may be baptized upon confession of faith if not previously baptized.	Adults only. Infants are incapable of faith; must reach conscious "age of accountability." Only adults are capable of repentance and faith. Infants are often "dedicated."	Infants, children and adults. Infants are baptized based on the covenant. They are baptized into future faith and repentance.

Additional notes:

- Anglicans, Episcopal, and Methodists also baptize infants.
- The Evangelical Free Church in America accepts both infant and adult baptism, after a decision in 1950. In practice, however, adult baptism is more common.
- Pentecostals generally baptize only adults, and only by immersion.
- Most "non-denominational" churches tend to be either Baptist or Pentecostal by doctrinal affiliation, and thus practice believers' baptism.

Statement of Faith of the Church of the Lutheran Brethren [11]

"The knowledge and benefits of Christ's redemption from sin is brought to the human race through the means of grace, namely the Word and the sacraments.

In the Sacrament of Baptism, God offers the benefits of Christ's redemption to all people and graciously bestows the washing of regeneration and newness of life to all who believe. God calls the baptized person to live in daily repentance, that is, in sorrow for sin, in turning from sin, and in personal faith in the forgiveness of sin obtained by Christ. By grace we are daily given the power to overcome sinful desires and live a new life in Christ. Those who do not continue to live in God's grace need to be brought again to repentance and faith through the Law and Gospel."

This is most certainly true…

334. What does the word baptism mean?

The English word baptism comes from the word in the Greek language which means a cleansing by washing, immersion, and/or a death.

338. What is Baptism?

Baptism is not merely water, but it is water used according to God's command and connected with God's Word.

339. What does it mean to be baptized in the name of the Father and of the Son and of the Holy Spirit?

It means that I have been brought into union with the Triune God, that I belong to Him, and that I bear His name.

340. Who should be baptized?

Everyone should be baptized because everyone needs the grace of God, including little children. (Matthew 28:19)

342. Can little children have faith?

Yes, little children can have faith because Jesus says that they believe. (Matthew 18:6)

343. Are baptized children saved?

Yes, baptized children are saved because Jesus has given each one of them the gift of faith, and they do not resist Him by unbelief.

344. How shall these baptized children be regarded?

They shall be regarded as children of God and encouraged to take their sins to Jesus and choose daily to follow Him.

351. What benefits did you receive when you were baptized?

1. My sin was forgiven. (Acts 2:38,39)
2. I was born again. (John 3:3,5; I Peter 3:20b, 21a; Mark 16:16; Titus 3:4-7)
3. God adopted me into His family, the church. (John 1:12; I Corinthians 12:12,13)
4. God established His covenant with me. (Colossians 2:10, 12; Galatians 3:26-29)
5. God gave me a way to live. (Romans 6:1-4)

Explanation of Luther's Small Catechism

Baptism and Conversion

Lutherans do not believe in the doctrine of Eternal Security; therefore they believe that it is possible for a baptized person, whether baptized as an infant or an adult, to turn away from his faith. For this reason the need for repentance and conversion is preached, as that is the only way back to a living faith in Christ. They also teach the necessity of a "conscious awakening" to the reality of sin and need for repentance, an awakening which must occur in a child as he comes to maturity. A number of Lutheran theologians address this issue clearly:

- ***Martin Luther***:

"To arise from sin and repent is nothing other than to return to the power of Baptism and to faith, from which we had fallen away, and to return to the promise which was given (by God) in Baptism, but which we had forsaken by our sin." [12]

- ***Dr. Erik Pontoppidan*** in his *Explanation of Luther's Small Catechism* (1737 A.D.):

"**Question 692:** Is a sinner regenerated again during his time of conversion, after he has lost the first regeneration grace in Baptism? **Answer**: Yes, every conversion from dead words and awakening to new life is a new birth. **Question 693**: Is not Baptism the only means of regeneration? **Answer**: No, the Word has the same power and effect." (I Peter 1:23) [13]

- **The Augsburg Confession, Article XII**:
"Of Repentance they teach that for those who have fallen after Baptism there is remission of sins whenever they are converted; and that the Church ought to impart absolution to those thus returning to repentance." [14]

- **O. Hallesby**, Norwegian theologian, in *Infant Baptism and Adult Conversion*:
"We must, in the first place, take exception to the idea that a baptized person retains a living germ of the Baptismal life within itself also when he is living in sin without acknowledging it and without honestly confessing it."[15] Professor Omar Gjerness, commenting on Hallesby's statement writes: "If the Lutheran church believed in the doctrine of eternal security, it would be apparent that there would be no place for evangelism within its baptized membership. But because Lutherans do believe that a person may fall from grace, and because they do believe that a life of faith is an essential concomitant of baptism, Lutherans may consistently evangelize both the baptized and the unbaptized." [16]

- **Uuras Saarnivaara**, in *Scriptural Baptism*:
"Sad to say, it is quite common in churches practicing infant baptism to lay emphasis on pure doctrine and external 'churchianity.' There is no call to conversion, devoted Christian life, and consecrated service. All that is required is that one learn his catechism, attend church services, partake of the Lord's Supper, contribute to the work of the church, and lead a decent life. All that is, of course, good and necessary; but a person may well have all that and still be entirely void of true knowledge of Christ and life in Him. When people are allowed to assume that they are Christians and heirs of eternal life without true repentance and faith, they are actually led to build up their own righteousness, and will finally be condemned." [17]

- **Carl F. Wisloff,** in *I Know in Whom I Believe*:
"Baptism is basic to the child's Christian life when he awakens to conscious faith. God's plan is that the child shall always remain with Jesus. But even if he turns away from Jesus, and later is converted to Him, the Word of promise in Baptism is always the basis for his standing in grace. Infant Baptism means that God was there with His call to grace as early as possible in the child's life, because He wants the entire life to be consecrated to Him. Therefore Baptism has properly been called the 'portal of grace.' In Baptism God gives the child all of His grace." Wisloff also described a transition period in which there must be a conscious awakening to an adult life in God, a time of crisis when his Christian faith becomes his adult possession. "A conscious choice and a new consciousness of wanting to belong to Jesus are necessary." [18]

- **Rev. A.A. Pedersen**, professor at Lutheran Brethren Seminary:
Pedersen answers the question, "**Do you believe it is possible for children who are baptized as infants and thus regenerated to continue to live with God in unbroken fellowship until their death?** Yes, we do. However, we also believe that before the fact of their salvation can be reality to them as a conscious life with God, they will need what we have called a crisis experience of sin and grace." And, "**Why must the faithful child have this experience?** Without it there is a very great danger that he will depend upon his own goodness for salvation and become a self-righteous Pharisee. He cannot enter into a conscious fellowship with God until sin and grace have become realities to him." [19]

Responses to Common Objections to Infant Baptism

1. Children are being baptized based on their parents' faith rather than their own.

Parents are bringing their children in contact with the One who brings them His grace, in much the same way that parents in the Old Testament brought their 8-day-old sons for circumcision, the friends brought their paralyzed friend to Jesus for healing (Matthew 9) and parents brought their little ones to Jesus (Mark 10). In another Old Testament picture, when the people of Israel were being bitten by snakes, Moses was instructed to erect a bronze serpent (snake) to which all who were bitten could look and they would be healed. Parents certainly must have turned their little ones' faces so they could look and be healed. It was not the parents' faith that would have brought healing to their children; it was faith in God's provision that moved them to place their unresisting children in contact with their salvation. (Number 21:8) Jesus relates this story to his own crucifixion when discussing Nicodemus' need for salvation, "Just as Moses lifted up the snake in the desert, so the Son of Man must be lifted up, that everyone who believes in him may have eternal life." (John 3:14)

2. The Bible nowhere states that infants should be baptized.

Neither does it prohibit them. In fact, Jesus was indignant with disciples who sought to prevent little children from coming to Him. Similarly, nowhere in Scripture does it say that the Lord's Supper should be given to women, but we would never deny them. It is assumed that they are included, just as it is assumed that the Great Commission is intended for all the world; all people.

***3.* Children cannot have faith until they are older and can understand and verbally respond to God's offer of salvation.**

Luke 18:15-17 and Mark 10:14 use the word "*brephos*" for children, which means "babes in arms," or "babies" (in the NIV). Jesus welcomed them. Some argue that He did not baptize them, He only blessed them. But what did He have to give them if not Himself? Further, baptism had not yet been instituted by Jesus. That occurred at the time of His ascension. Faith is a gift, not dependant on age or intellect, but on trust and dependence, as a little child. (Matthew 18:1-6; I Peter 2:2, Mark 9:36-37)

4. In Acts, baptism always followed repentance and conversion.

In many cases it did, as these were adults who were being converted (the Ethiopian eunuch in Acts. 8:36; Saul in Acts 22:16, for example). There were also entire households who were baptized, and it is nearly impossible to believe that these households did not include babies and young children. (Lydia's household: Acts 16:15; the Philippian jailor's household: Acts 16:33; the household of Stephanas. (I Corinthians 1:16)

5. Baptism is pictured in the Bible as being "buried and resurrected in Christ." Therefore immersion would be the only method to depict that, and infants would never be submerged in water.

No ceremonial baptism in which any form of the word "bapto" is used in the Old Testament implies immersion. It is clearly pouring. (Exodus 22:22; Leviticus 4:6, 9:9; Daniel 4:30; Numbers 19:18). The amount of water and the method of its use is not the important issue.

***6.* The early church only practiced immersion.**

Many early church fathers mention infant baptism, and archaeological data also depict the practice of pouring water in baptism.

***7.* Children are not accountable to God for their sins until they reach an age of understanding and can choose to either accept or reject Christ.**

Infants are under the curse of the fall and need salvation. (Romans 3:10-28; Romans 5:12-21)

8. **Scripture says in Mark 10:14 that children belong to the Kingdom of God.**

Actually that verse indicates that the Kingdom belongs *to children*; it should not be denied to them.

Because you asked…

***1.* Where does the Bible teach that sin is forgiven in baptism?**

I Peter 3:21; Galatians 3:27; Titus 3:5-6; Romans 6:3, John 3:5; I Corinthians 6:11; Colossians 2:11-12; Acts 2:38; Acts 22:16, Ephesians 5:26.

2. If a child dies before he is baptized, is he lost?

"To this we would briefly reply that the very men who drew up our confessions deny emphatically that it is thus absolutely necessary. Luther, Melanchthon, Bugenhagen and others, repudiate the idea that an unbaptized infant is lost. No single acknowledged theologian of the Lutheran Church ever taught this repulsive doctrine."[20] Pastors were instructed to point parents to the word of Jesus: "It is not the will of your Father who is heaven that one of these little ones perish." (Matthew 18:14) Parents are to be responsible for what the Bible instructs them to do and the rest is left to a loving God.

3. If sin is forgiven in baptism can a person still be lost in later life?

The Explanation to Luther's Small Catechism states in answer to **Question 357**: "Yes, a baptized person can fall away from God by resisting or ignoring the Holy Spirit and by neglecting prayer, the Bible, and the Lord's Supper." (I Timothy 1:18b, 19a; II Timothy 4:3, 4; Hebrews 3:12). And in **Question 358** in answer to how such a person can be restored: "The Holy Spirit restores all those who repent of sin and believe the promises that God has given." (I John 1:9; Isaiah 55:6, 7; Revelation 3:20.) Should he then be re-baptized? "No, God has not gone back on His Word. By confession of sin a person may return to fellowship with God." (Romans 3:3,4a, **Question 359**.)

4. **Isn't dedicating children, as other Protestants practice, just the same as baptizing them?**

No, it is not the sacrament that includes the water and the Word, as instituted by Christ.

5. What does "Age of Accountability" mean?

It is a term used by those who do not practice infant baptism to describe a period or age when they believe a child is able to understand and confess his sin, verbalize his need for salvation, and thus be held "accountable" for either accepting or rejecting Christ's work of salvation. The term is never used in Scripture.

6. **Should an adult ever be re-baptized in order to join a church that practices only believers' baptism**?

No, baptism is a one-time sacrament, a work that God does for us, not that we do for Him. (Ephesians 4:5, "*...one Lord, one faith, one baptism, one God and Father of all, who is over all and through all and in all.*")

7. **What is the role of sponsors in baptism?**

They are to teach, pray for, and encourage the child's faith, in obedience to Christ's Great Commission command both to baptize and to teach. The congregation is also considered to be responsible for the spiritual care of the child who is baptized into the body of Christ.

For further reading and study: *Understanding Four Views on Baptism*, John H. Armstrong editor. This helpful book includes presentations and responses of each view, all instances of the use of the word baptism in the New Testaments, statements on baptism in Creeds, Confessions and Catechisms; quotations about baptism from Augustine and other church fathers, reformers , and diverse theologians as well as four pages of resources; *We Believe* by Tim Ysteboe; *I Know In Whom I Believe* by Carl F. Wisloff; *The Christian Faith* by Robert Kolb; *Baptism and Related Doctrines* by Omar Gjerness; two brochures by Faith and Fellowship Publishing: *Modes and Meaning of Baptism* (Johnson) and *Did the Apostles Practice Infant Baptism?* (Stone); *Systematic Theology* by Wayne Grudem; *Why Be Baptized*? by Rose Publishing. (see Bibliography)

Endnotes:

---

1. Walter Wangerin, "Maundy Thursday", in Eugene H. Peterson and Emilie Griffin, eds. *Epiphanies: Stories for the Christian Year* (Grand Rapids: Baker Books, 2003), 124.
2. Tim Ysteboe, *We Believe: A Commentary on the Statement of Faith* (Fergus Falls, MN: Faith & Fellowship Publishing, 2009), 104-105.
3. Alister E. McGrath, gen. ed., *Zondervan Handbook of Christian Beliefs* (Grand Rapids: Zondervan, 2005), 247.
4. Johann Rist, *The Concordia Hymnal* (Minneapolis: Augsburg Publishing House, 1933), 90
5. McGrath, *Zondervan Handbook of Christian Beliefs*, 243.
6. John H. Armstrong, *Understanding Four Views on Baptism* (Grand Rapids: Zondervan, 2007), 12. Counterpoints Church Life Series, Paul E. Engle, series ed.
7. Martin Luther, in *Luther's Large Catechism*. Quoted in John H. Armstrong, *Understanding Four Views on Baptism,* 190-191.
8. J. B. Lightfoot , orig. ed.; J. R. Harmer, ed., comp., "The Apostolic Fathers". Reprint. (Grand Rapids: Baker, 1956), 126. Cited in Paul Enns, *The Moody Handbook of Theology* (Chicago: Moody Publishers, 2008), 375.
9. Arnold M. Stone, *Did the Apostles Practice Infant Baptism?* (Fergus Falls, MN: Faith & Fellowship Publishing, 1983), 2-3.
10. William Whiting, "O Lord, Our Little Ones to Thee", in *The Concordia Hymnal* (Minneapolis: Augsburg Publishing House, 1933), 83.
11. *Doctrinal Statement of Faith—Church of the Lutheran Brethren, Article II G2, 2012.* Available as a pamphlet at www.faithandfellowship.org.

12. Martin Luther, quoted in Carl F. Wisloff, *I Know In Whom I Believe: Studies in Bible Doctrine*. Rev. Karl Stendal, trans. (Minneapolis: AFLC Seminary Press, 1983), 114.
13. Dr. Erik Pontoppidan, quoted in Carl F. Wisloff, *I Know In Whom I Believe*, 114.
14. *Concordia Triglotta*, (St. Louis: Concordia Publishing House, 1921), 49.
15. O. Hallesby, *Infant Baptism and Adult Conversion* (Minneapolis: Messenger Press, 1947), 60
16. Omar Gjerness, *Baptism & Related Doctrines* (Fergus Falls, MN: Faith & Fellowship Publishing, 1982), 39.
17. Uuras Saarnivaara, *Scriptural Baptism* (New York: Vantage Press, 1953), 68. Quoted in Gjerness, *Baptism & Related Doctrines*, 47.
18. Carl F. Wisloff, *I Know In Whom I Believe: Studies in Bible Doctrine*. Rev. Karl Stendal, trans. (Minneapolis: AFLC Seminary Press, 1983), 112-113.
19. A. A. Pedersen, quoted in Dale Varberg, *Faith and Fellowship: A Look at Lutheran Brethren Theology 1900-2000.* (Fergus Falls, MN: Faith & Fellowship Publishing, 2000), 152.
20. G. H. Gerberding, *The Way of Salvation in the Lutheran Church* (Minneapolis: Augsburg Publishing House, 1919). Quoted in Tim Ysteboe, *We Believe: A Commentary on the Statement of Faith* (Fergus Falls, MN: Faith & Fellowship Publishing, 2009), 110.

Chapter 7

Life After Life: The Doctrine of Heaven and Hell

Life After Life

The Doctrine of Heaven and Hell

After my husband, Bruce, went home to be with the Lord in 2005, I found great comfort in the Word, in the care and kindness of my family and friends, and in the body of believers in the church. The Lord Himself ministered comfort and hope to me in the hours of the night as Scriptures and hymns wove themselves into my troubled thoughts. But I also found that I had questions about heaven which I'd never thought of before:

Where is heaven, really?

What will our relationship be when I arrive, too? I know there is no marriage in heaven—but certainly the God who united us as one in this life will not separate us in eternity, will He? I had always thought of us as "bruceandruth" and couldn't imagine the joy of heaven without sharing it with my soul-mate.

What form is he in now, if his body is here but his soul is there?

Is he conscious and aware of us?

I would look up into the star-filled sky at night and say to Bruce, "I don't know where you are in all of this, but I KNOW who you are with!" That gave me joy!

Then the Lord brought me to this verse:

"Dear friends, now we are children of God, [identity] and what we will be has not yet been made known. [mystery] But we know that when He appears, we shall be like Him [certainty] because we shall see Him just as He is. And every one who has this hope fixed on Him purifies himself, just as He is pure." [sanctity] (I John 3:2-3)

I came to accept the mystery: that there was much that I could never comprehend about all that God has prepared for His children. I embraced the purpose in my heart to commit myself fully to the Lord, asking His strength to remain in living faith, in the gracious state of conscious repentance, forgiveness and renewal. But I also set about learning as much as I could about heaven.

This is most certainly true…

***195.* What benefits do you have because of the resurrection of Christ?**

1. The resurrection assures me that Jesus is the Son of God. (Rom. 1:4)
2. The resurrection assures me that Jesus has fully paid for my sins. (Rom. 4:25)
3. The resurrection gives me power to arise from spiritual death, and to live a new life. (Rom. 6:4)
4. The resurrection assures me that I shall rise on the last day. (I Cor. 15:20,21) *- Explanation of Luther's Small Catechism*

"I must keep alive in myself the desire for my true country, which I shall not find till after death; I must never let it get snowed under or turned aside; I must make it the main object of life to press on to that other country and to help others do the same." [1]
C.S. Lewis

"Our greatest affliction is not anxiety, or even guilt, but rather homesickness—a nostalgia or ineradicable yearning to be at home with God." [2]
- Donald Bloesch

"When I get to heaven, I shall see three wonders there. The first wonder will be to see many there whom I did not expect to see; the second wonder will be to miss many people who I did expect to see; and the third and greatest wonder of all will be to find myself there." [3]
John Newton

What happens when we die?

Peter Kreeft and Ronald K. Tacelli, in *Handbook of Christian Apologetics*, state six basic theories about what happens to people when they die. For a clear and extensive discussion and refutation of the non-Christian views, see pages 227-258 of this very helpful book. [4]

Materialism	Nothing survives; death ends everything. It is the natural belief resulting from atheism.
Paganism	A "vague, shadowy semi-self or ghost survives and goes to the place of the dead, or underworld. It is the standard pagan belief...the 'ghost' that survives is less alive, less substantial, less real than the flesh and blood organism now living." (p. 227)
Reincarnation	The individual soul survives and is reincarnated (takes residence) in another body. Karma is the belief that after the soul has fulfilled its destiny and learned its lessons and has become sufficiently enlightened, it reverts to a divine status or is absorbed into the divine ALL.
Pantheism	"Death changes nothing; what survives death is the same as what was real before death: only the one, changeless, eternal, perfectly spiritual, divine all-inclusive Reality, sometimes called by a name ('Brahman') and sometimes not (as in Buddhism)." This is the view of Eastern mysticism. "We are drops of the cosmic ocean, pieces of God-stuff. At death the drop returns to the sea; there is no real individuality." (p. 260)
Immortality	"The individual soul survives death, but not the body. This soul eventually reaches its eternal destiny of heaven or hell, perhaps through intermediate stages, perhaps through reincarnation. But what survives is an individual, bodiless spirit. This is Platonism, often confused with Christianity." (p. 227)
Resurrection	"At death the soul separates from the body and is reunited at the end of the world to its new, immortal, resurrected body by a divine miracle. This is the Christian view." (p. 228)

What is heaven like?

- It is a PLACE: "Do not let your hearts be troubled. Trust in God; trust also in me. In my Father's house are many rooms; if it were not so, I would have told you. I am going there to prepare a place for you. And if I go and prepare a place for you, I will come back and take you to be with me that you also may be where I am." (John 14:1-3)
- It is built by God, and is PERMANENT: "Now we know that if the earthly tent we live in is destroyed, we have a building from God, an eternal house in heaven, not built by human hands." (II Corinthians. 5:1)
- JESUS is there! Stephen, the first Christian martyr, saw Him, "Stephen, full of the Holy Spirit, looked up to heaven and saw the glory of God, and Jesus standing at the right hand of God. 'Look," he said, 'I see heaven open and the Son of Man standing at the right hand of God.'" (Acts 7:55-56) . Jesus also, while dying on the cross, promised to the repentant thief beside him, "Today you will be with me in paradise." (Luke 23:43)

Six earthly activities that continue in heaven because they are the reason we are here on earth and are rarely if ever completed here, are described by Peter Kreeft in *Everything You Ever Wanted to Know About Heaven.* They relate to two human activities (knowing and loving) that come from the soul, not the body, and separate us from animals.

1. Understanding God
2. Loving God
3. Understanding others
4. Loving others
5. Understanding yourself
6. Loving yourself

Kreeft declares, "All earthly art, love, poetry, philosophy, theology, music, liturgy, and loving deeds probably resemble their heavenly fruit about as much as a watermelon seed resembles a watermelon...Even on earth these are the six things that are inexhaustible and non-boring. They are our dress rehearsal for heaven." [5]

For thoughtful answers to questions you probably have about heaven, (How can we know anything about heaven? How can I be happy in heaven if loved ones are in hell? If we will all be perfect saints in heaven, where will individuality be?), Kreeft addresses twenty-nine on pages 263-278. Randy Alcorn, in his popular book, *Heaven*, also provides helpful teaching on the theology of heaven, questions and answers about heaven, and living in light of heaven.

"I used to think, loving life so greatly, that to die would be like leaving the party before the end. But now I know that the party is really happening somewhere else . . . and that the light and the music escaping in snatches to make the pulse beat faster and the tempo quicken comes from another place...and I know, too, when I get there, that the music and the love and the praise will belong to Him, and the music will never end." [7]
Bob Bensen

Where is heaven?

The word "heaven" is used three ways in the Bible:

Atmospheric heaven—the space surrounding earth (Deut. 33:13, Job 38:29, Isaiah 55:10, I Samuel 2:10, Psalm 147:8)

Celestial heaven—the universe (Genesis 1:1, Psalm 33:6)

The home of God—Matthew 6:9, Psalm 2:4, Isaiah 66:1, Deut. 26:15)

Heaven is also called "paradise" (II Corinthians 12:4), and the Bible teaches that there is an "intermediate" heaven where believers who have died live until they receive their resurrected bodies at Christ's return to the earth. Paul Enns, in *The Moody Handbook of Theology*, states, "Although believers will not receive their resurrection bodies until the rapture, it is apparent that believers will have bodies in the intermediate state in heaven." [6] He makes the case that Moses and Elijah, who appeared with Christ to the disciples at the Transfiguration.

"If I find in myself a desire which no experience in this world can satisfy, the most probable explanation is that I was made for another world . . . At present, we are on the outside of the world, the wrong side of the door. But all the leaves of the NT are rustling with the rumor that it will not always be so. Some day, God willing, we shall get in." [8]
C.S. Lewis

(Matt. 17:3-4) were recognizable, and that in Jesus' story about the rich man and Lazarus (Luke 16:19-31), Lazarus appears in bodily form, reclining next to Abraham.

The Word also teaches us that there will one day be a new heaven and earth, the final dwelling place of believers. Some see this as an entirely new creation (II Peter 3:10), and some see it as a renewed earth, restored to the glory it had before the fall of man into sin.

Who will be in heaven?

Jesus promises that all who truly believe in Him have eternal life and will be with Him in heaven:

John 3:16: "For God so loved the world, that He gave His only begotten Son, that whosoever believeth in Him should not perish, but have everlasting life." (KJV)

John 5:24: "I tell you the truth, whoever hears my word and believes Him who sent me has eternal life and will not be condemned; he has crossed over from death to life."

John 11:25-26: "I am the resurrection and the life. He who believes in me will live, even though he dies; and whoever lives and believes in me will never die."

"I am standing at the seashore. A ship at my side spreads her white sails to the morning breeze and starts for the blue ocean. I stand and watch her until, at length, she hangs like a speck of white cloud, just where the sea and sky come to mingle with each other . . . and just at the moment when someone at my side says, 'There, she is gone!' there are other eyes watching her coming and other voices ready to take up the glad shout 'Here she comes!' And that is dying."[9]
Henry VanDyke

In response to Thomas' question to Jesus, "Lord, we don't know where you are going, so how can we know the way?" Jesus answered in John 14: 6, "I am the way and the truth and the life. No one comes to the Father except through me."

And David expresses his confidence, "With Thy counsel Thou wilt guide me, and afterward receive me to glory." (Psalm 73:24) and "Surely goodness and mercy shall follow me all the days of my life: and I will dwell in the house of the Lord forever." (Psalm 23:6)

How shall I live as I await my new home?

1. With motivation to share the Good News of salvation through Jesus for all people! "We are Christ's ambassadors, as though God were making his appeal through us. We implore you on Christ's behalf: Be reconciled to God." (II Corinthians. 5:20)
2. With confidence. "We are always confident and know that as long as we are at home in the body we are away from the Lord...We are confident, I say, and would prefer to be away from the body and at home with the Lord." (II Corinthians. 6-8)
3. With anticipation and longing. "Meanwhile we groan, longing to be clothed with our heavenly dwelling." (II Corinthians. 5:2)
4. With purpose. "So we make it our goal to please Him, whether we are at home in the body or away from it." (II Corinthians. 5:9) "Christ's love compels us, because we are convinced that one died for all, and therefore all died. And He died for all, that those who live should no longer live for themselves but for Him who died for them and was raised again."
5. With reality, but release from fear: "Though I walk through the valley of the shadow of death I will fear no evil for You are with me, Your rod and Your staff they comfort me." (Psalm 23:4)

Confident Christians

Alice Macdonald Kipling, the mother of the famous author Rudyard Kipling, penned this lovely poem describing the marvelous new Day which awaits believers in Jesus.

As from my window at first glimpse of dawn
    I watch the rising mist that heralds day.
And see by God's strong hand the curtain drawn
    That through the night has hid the world away;
So I, through windows of my soul shall see
    One day Death's fingers with resistless might
Draw back the curtained gloom that shadows life,
    And on the darkness of time's deepest night,
Let in the perfect Day—Eternity. [10]

What are some false views of heaven?

- ***Purgatory,*** described as an intermediate stage after death in which those who have died in a state of grace are given a chance to "purge" themselves of sin before going to heaven. This view has no basis in Scripture, but Catholics in particular teach the doctrine based on the Apocryphal book of 2 Maccabees 12:39-45. The Reformers rejected this teaching because there was no foundation in Scripture and because it wasn't consistent with the doctrine of justification by faith alone.

- "***All roads lead to heaven***," the assertion that what really matters is sincerity and moral character; that there is no one absolute truth about the way to heaven. Jesus, however, emphatically stated in John 14:6, "I am the way, the truth, and the life. No one comes to the Father except through me." And Acts 4:12 could not be any clearer: "Salvation is found in no one else, for there is no other name under heaven given to men by which we must be saved." To believe that there are alternate paths is to deny the total truth and accuracy (inerrancy) of the Word of God—which many do.

- ***Prayer for the dead*** (Catholic practice), or being baptized for the dead (Mormon practice). There is no Scriptural foundation for any change in spiritual condition after death.

- ***"Soul sleep"***, the belief that when Christians die they go into an unconscious state. It is based on some passages that refer to death as "sleep" (Matt. 9:24, 27:52), though that should be seen as a metaphor.

- ***Fantasy:*** "They're looking down on us," "They are our angels." These may bring a degree of comfort to the grief-stricken, but are not Scriptural and are romanticized ideas.

For further study of some of these views, see extensive sections both in Wayne Grudem's *Systematic Theology*, Paul Enn's *Moody Handbook of Theology* and most other comprehensive systematic theology texts.

My Heart is Longing to Praise My Savior

Princess Eugenie of Sweden, tr. P.A. Sveeggen, Norwegian Folk-Tune.

My heart is longing to praise my Savior, and glorify His name in song and prayer.
For He has shown me His wondrous favor, and offered me all heaven with Him to share.

I walked in blindness; my soul was dying; The prince of darkness held me in his power.
In pain I turned to my Father crying; He broke my chains and saved me in that hour.

O blessed Jesus, what Thou hast given, through dying on the cross in bitter pain,
Has filled my heart with the peace of heaven; my winter's gone and spring is mine again.

O Christian friends, let our song ascending, give honor, praise to Him who set us free!
Our tribulations may seem unending; but soon with Him we shall forever be.

Soon we are home and shall stand before Him; what matter then tho' we have suffered here.
Then He shall crown us, while we adorn Him; so death and all our pains will disappear.

To Thee, O Savior, our adoration shall rise forever for Thy precious blood
Which blotted out all the accusation of sin and guilt which once against us stood.

What blessed joy overflows my spirit, because Thy wondrous grace was granted me.
Thy work complete, that I may inherit at last eternal life in heaven with Thee! [11]

What is hell?

Terms

Hell: The place of final, eternal, conscious punishment for those who have not responded in repentance and faith to God's offer of salvation through His Son Jesus.

Hades: A place for the spirits of the dead between death and final punishment or reward; a NT term for the afterlife, equivalent to Sheol. (see *Explanation of Luther's Small Catechism,* #194)

Sheol: In the OT, variously translated "grave", or "hell."

Gehenna: A designation for eternal punishment.

Abyss: Meaning "bottomless pit", where Satan will be sent during Jesus millennial reign on the earth. (Luke 8:31; Rev. 20:1-3)

Other descriptions in the Bible:
"unquenchable fire" - (Matthew 3:12)
"outer darkness" - (Matthew 8:12)
"lake of fire" - (Revelation 21:8)

"It would be dreadful to suffer this fierceness and wrath of Almighty God for one moment; but you must suffer it for all eternity. There will be no end to this exquisite horrible misery...You will know that you must wear out long ages, millions of millions of ages, in wrestling and conflicting with this almighty merciless vengeance." [12]

Jonathan Edwards
(1703-58)

What is hell like?

- It is eternal. Matthew 25:30: "*Cast the worthless servant into the outer darkness; there men will weep and gnash their teeth.* Matthew 25:41, "*Depart from me, you cursed, into the eternal fire prepared for the devil and his angels.*" Jesus says (verse 46) they "*will go away into eternal punishment but the righteous into eternal life.*"

- It is conscious. In Jesus' story of the rich man and Lazarus (Luke 16:22-24, 28) the rich man describes his state in hell as "*this place of torment,*" In Revelation 14: 9-11 the state of the damned is described, "*The smoke of their torment goes up forever and ever; and they have no rest, day or night, these worshipers of the beast and its image.*" The word translated "punishment" in Matthew 25:46 is *kolasis,* used to describe terrible physical torture endured by persecuted believers, in the writings of the church fathers, Polycarp and Ignatius.

"When we preach on hell, we might at least do it with tears in our eyes."[13]
D.L. Moody

- It is separation. It is total separation from God, total absence of His favor and blessing.

> "Because the doctrine of eternal conscious punishment is so foreign to the thought patterns of our culture, and, on a deeper level, to our instinctive and God-given sense of love and desire for redemption for every human being created in God's image, this doctrine is emotionally one of the most difficult doctrines for Christians to affirm today. It also tends to be one of the first doctrines given up by people who are moving away from a commitment to the Bible as absolutely truthful in all that it affirms. Among liberal theologians who do not accept the absolute truthfulness of the Bible, there is probably no one today who believes in the doctrine of eternal conscious punishment." [14]

False teachings about hell:

Annihilation: A belief that after the wicked have suffered punishment for a time, they will no longer exist. Seventh Day Adventists, and others hold this view.

Conditional immortality: The teaching that God has created people so that they only have immortality if they accept salvation through Christ. Those who do not become Christians will just cease to exist at death or at the final judgment. But, of course, that would remove any idea of justice or punishment, which is contrary to Scripture.

"The safest road to hell is the gradual one—The gentle slope, soft underfoot, without sudden turnings, without milestones, without signposts." [15]
C.S. Lewis

In light of this truth, what should a believer's attitude be?

- Sorrow for the lost

Paul, in Romans 9:2 wrote, "I have great sorrow and unceasing anguish in my heart. For I could wish that I myself were cursed and cut off from Christ for the sake of my brothers...the people of Israel."

Jesus, weeping over the lost of Jerusalem said, "Oh Jerusalem, Jerusalem, you who kill the prophets and stone those sent to you, how often I have longed to gather your children together, as a hen gathers her chicks under her wings, but you were not willing." (Matt. 23:37)

God, pleading with His people, declared, "As I live says the Lord God, I have no pleasure in the death of the wicked, but that the wicked turn from his way and live. Turn back, turn back from your evil ways; for why will you die, O house of Israel?" (Ezekiel 33:11)

- Urgency to spread the Good News

Sin, which leads to this terrifying punishment, has been fully paid for by the sacrifice of Jesus. Romans 6:23 states, "The wages of sin is death, but the gift of God is eternal life in Christ Jesus our Lord." Believers have Good News to share with lost people!

- Confidence in God

Rev. Robert Overgaard, past president of the Church of the Lutheran Brethren notes, "The cross reveals the extent to which God has gone in order to seek and to save the lost. God's suffering to remove the sin barrier so that people can be justly made right with Himself clearly shows His heart. Since God did not 'spare His own Son, but delivered Him up for us all,' we can trust Him in the final judgment in all matters we cannot now fully anticipate, nor understand." [16]

"Enter through the narrow gate. For wide is the gate and broad is the road that leads to destruction, and many enter through it. But small is the gate and narrow the road that leads to life, and only a few find it." - Jesus, in Matthew 7:13

Endnotes:

1. C. S. Lewis, quoted in Randy Alcorn, *Heaven* (Carol Stream, IL: Tyndale House Publishers, 2004), 439.
2. Donald Bloesch, *Theological Notebook* (Colorado Springs: Helmers and Howard, 1989), 183.
3. John Newton, quoted in Alister E. McGrath, *Zondervan Handbook of Christian Beliefs* (Grand Rapids: Zondervan, 2005), 285.
4. Peter Kreeft and Ronald Tacelli, *Handbook of Christian Apologetics* (Downers Grove, IL: InterVarsity Press, 1994), 227-258.
5. Ibid., 263, 271.
6. Paul Enns, *The Moody Handbook of Theology* (Chicago: Moody Publishers, 2008), 387.
7. Bob Bensen, quoted in "Heaven", DVD by Gaither Gospel Series, Springhouse/EMI, 2003.
8. C. S. Lewis, *A Year With C. S. Lewis: Daily Readings from His Classic Works*. (New York: HarperCollins, 2003), 397.
9. Variously attributed to Henry Scott Holland and Henry VanDyke. Source uncertain. Cited in Randy Alcorn, *Heaven*, 446.
10. Alice Macdonald Kipling, quoted in *Women's Devotional Bible, NIV* (Grand Rapids: Zondervan, 1990), 1391.

11. Princess Eugenie of Sweden, tr. P.A. Sveeggen, 1931, *The Concordia Hymnal* (Minneapolis: Augsburg Publishing House, 1933), 26. I have included this very old, beautiful hymn of praise and the hope of heaven, as it was my mother's favorite hymn, and mine as well.
12. Jonathan Edwards, "Sinners in the Hands of an Angry God", Sermon preached at Enfield, July 8, 1741. (Salem, MA: G.Roulstrone, 1st ser., no. 19618).
13. D. L. Moody, cited in Paul Enns, *The Moody Handbook of Theology,* 237.
14. Wayne Grudem, *Systematic Theology: An Introduction to Biblical Doctrine* (Grand Rapids: Zondervan.1994), 1152.
15. C. S. Lewis, *The Screwtape Letters* (New York: HarperCollins, 2001, first published in 1920).
16. Robert Overgaard, Sr., in personal correspondence. Used by permission.

Chapter 8

Last Things: The Return of Jesus Christ

Last Things: the Return of Jesus Christ

"Behold, I am coming soon! My reward is with me, and I will give to everyone according to what he has done. I am the Alpha and the Omega, the First and the Last, the Beginning and the End...He who testifies to these things says, 'Yes, I am coming soon.' Amen. Come, Lord Jesus."

Revelation 22:12-13,20

I was still a teenager when I discovered this short verse by Horatius Bonar which I inscribed in my Bible and have kept in my heart for decades:

Let nothing disturb thee, nothing afright thee.
All things are passing, God never changes.
Whom God possesses in nothing is anxious.
Alone God suffices.

Horatius Bonar, a great 19th century hymn writer, lived a life of confident faith in Jesus Christ though he suffered greatly in his personal life. Five of his children died in quick succession, leaving his family in sorrow but also comforted by the hope of Christ's return. He wrote, "We are but as wayfaring men, wandering in the lonely night, who see dimly upon the distant mountain peak the reflection of a sun that never rises here, but which shall never set in the 'new heavens' thereafter. And this is enough. It comforts and cheers us on our dark and rugged way." [1]

This great hope of Christ's promised return to earth has brought joy to believers from the first disciples down through the centuries. All true Christians agree on many things regarding this promise:

- Christ is coming back to earth, personally and visibly.
- His return will be preceded by signs which Jesus gave us.
- The dead will be raised.
- Sin will be judged.
- No one knows the exact time of His coming.

"When the Author walks on to the stage, the play is over…
It will be too late, then, to choose your side. There is no use saying you choose to lie down when it has become impossible to stand up." [2]
-C.S. Lewis

There is disagreement, though, on the details and the order of events of His return: Will there be a Great Tribulation? Will He come first to "rapture" believers before the time of the Tribulation? Will there be a literal 1,000-year reign of Christ on the earth? Does Revelation speak of the future of the nation of Israel or does it refer only to the Church, the bride of Christ?

Terms for better understanding

Eschatology. The study of the "last things," from the Greek word "eschatos," meaning "last." Theologians speak of "personal eschatology," meaning future things that will occur for individuals, while "general eschatology" refers to future events that the Bible teaches will affect all of the universe.

Second Coming. The return to earth that Christ promised in John 14:1-3 and which is prophesied elsewhere in Scripture.

Rapture. A term not used in the Bible, but an event which many believe will occur when believers will be caught up to heaven prior to the tribulation, as described in I Thessalonians 4:16-17. It will be sudden, and will come as "a thief in the night."

Tribulation, or the Great Tribulation. A period of intense suffering and trouble that will cover the earth in the end times. (Matthew 24:21; Revelation 6:15-17)

Antichrist. A false christ who will appear on the earth, deceiving many and gaining great, evil power during the tribulation. (I John 2:18)

Millennium. A period of 1,000 years during which Christ will rule on the earth following his return. It will be a time of great peace and prosperity, but will culminate with a final rebellion against God, ushering in final judgment. (Revelation 20:6) Theologians disagree both on the meaning and the timeline of the millennium.

Signs of Christ's Return

Dr. Wayne Grudem lists at least six signs which Scripture declares will occur before Christ's return. These do not mean, however, that Christ could not return suddenly, at any time. (Matthew 24:42-44, Mark 13:32-33; Luke 12:40; I Thessalonians 5:2, James 5:7-9; I Peter 4:7)

1. The preaching of the gospel to all nations (Mark 13:10; Matthew 24:14)
2. The Great Tribulation (Mark 13:7-8; Matthew 24:15-22; Luke 21:20-24)
3. False prophets working signs and wonders (Mark 13:22; Matthew 24:23-24)
4. Signs in the heavens (Mark 13:24-25; Matthew 24:29-30; Luke 21:25-27)
5. The coming of the man of sin (sometimes called "antichrist") and the rebellion (2 Thessalonians 2:1-10)
6. The salvation of Israel (Romans 11:25-26)[3]

Four Major Views of the End Times

Amillennialism. There will be no literal millennium (1,000-year reign of Christ on the earth). It is symbolic of Christ's reign in the lives of His people throughout the centuries until His second coming.

Postmillennialism. Christ will return after the millennium—a period during which the world gradually becomes better and better under the spread of the Gospel. This view was more widely accepted prior to the 20th century with its terrible wars, destruction, and disillusionment with man's ability to improve on human nature.

Historic Premillennialism. There will be a literal millennial reign of Christ. It will be ushered in by His second coming to earth. Believers will be on the earth during the tribulation period, usually considered to be seven years. (Revelation 7:14)

Dispensational Premillennialism There will be a literal millennial reign of Christ upon His return to earth following the Great Tribulation, but believers will have been "raptured" prior to the tribulation.

Comparative Views of End Times

Note: This information is gathered from many sources and is explained well in many texts, but Rose Publishing's "*Four Views of the End Times*" is particularly helpful. (see bibliography)

	Amillennialism	**Postmillennial-ism**	**Historic Premillennialism**	**Dispensational Premillennialism**
Second coming of Christ	Can come at any time.	Will come after the millennium.	Will come after a 7-year tribulation, and before the millennium.	Will come after a 7-year tribulation and before the millennium.
Rapture of the church	Occurs at the same time as Christ's second coming.	Occurs at the same time as Christ's second coming.	Occurs at the same time as Christ's second coming.	Church is first raptured before the tribulation or mid-tribulation. Christ returns fol-lowing the tribula-tion.
Great Tribula-tion	No. It occurs now during perse-cution.	No. It occurs now as the conflict be-tween good and evil.	A 7-year period, which believers will live through.	A 7-year period, but church is rap-tured either before or during it.
Millennium reign of Christ	No. He is reign-ing during the church age in hearts of believ-ers.	No. Present age becomes the mil-lennium as the Gospel spreads to all people.	Yes	Yes. Ushered in at time of second coming of Christ.
Israel/the Church	Church is the new Israel. Prophecy does not refer to the nation of Is-rael.	Church is the new Israel. Prophecy does not refer to the nation of Is-rael.	Church is the new Israel.	God has a plan for both the nation of Israel as well as the church.
Prominent theo-logians and writ-ers who hold/ held this view	Many believe that Augustine (354-430) was the first to support this view. Also Martin Luther and John Calvin; modern theologians such as Abraham Kuyper, Stanley Grenz, J.I. Packer; most Lutherans	Jonathan Edwards, Charles Haddon Spurgeon, B.B. Warfield, Augus-tus H. Strong, Charles Hodge, R.C. Sproul	Many early church fathers (Irenaeus, 130-200; Justin Martyr, 100-165) and others. Mod-ern teachers in-clude John War-wick Montgom-ery, Robert Gun-dry, George E. Ladd, M.J. Erickson	J. Nelson Darby, C.I. Scofield, Harry A. Ironside, Gleason Archer, Donald G. Barnhouse, Hal Lindsey, D.L. Moody, John MacArthur, Charles Ryrie, Charles Stanley, Norman Geisler, Tim LaHaye J.F. Walvoord

View of the Church of the Lutheran Brethren

While most Lutherans accept the amillennial view (see Robert Kolb, *The Christian Faith,* and others), other Lutherans are premillenial (see Carl F. Wisloff in *I Know in Whom I Believe,* as well as others). The Lutheran Brethren Position Paper, "Teaching About the Last Things," which was approved by the Synodical Council in 1997, states, "The literal second advent of Christ is a fundamental doctrine of the Christian faith clearly taught by our Lord and accepted by all orthodox Christians affirming the authority of Scripture, but any specific interpretation of the chronology surrounding the events of Christ's return is not a fundamental doctrine...We affirm that Scripture teaches that Christ will reign 1,000 years and that the Church of the Lutheran Brethren's primary tradition is premillennial, while allowing for other interpretations. Our premillennial tradition will be taught in our schools and churches. We deny that Scripture sets forth every detail of the nature of Christ's reign with minute precision." [4]

The Believer's Attitude Towards Christ's Promised Return

- **Expectant.** "When these things begin to take place, look up and raise your heads, because your redemption is drawing near." (Luke 21:28)

- **Alert.** "No one knows about that day or hour, not even the angels in heaven, nor the Son, but only the Father. Be on guard! Be alert! You do not know when that time will come...If he comes suddenly, do not let him find you sleeping. (Mark 13:32-33, 36)

- **Wise in use of time and treasure**. "Since everything will be destroyed in this way, what kind of people ought you to be? You ought to live holy and godly lives as you look forward to the day of God and speed its coming." (2 Peter 3:11-12) "Do not store up for yourselves treasures on earth, where moth and rust destroy, and where thieves break in and steal. But store up for yourselves treasures in heaven…for where your treasure is, there your heart will be also." (Matthew 6:19-21)

> "Turning. Serving. Waiting. These are the essentials of Christian conversion. We turn from the various idols of our lives with a decisive break from the past. We serve the living God with the gifts we have been given, experiencing liberation in the present. And we wait for Christ, looking to the future with hopeful expectancy. Without this turning, serving and waiting one can scarcely claim to have been converted." [5]
> - John Stott

- **Diligent to serve, motivated to spread the Gospel.** "Therefore, my dear brothers, stand firm. Let nothing move you. Always give yourselves fully to the work of the Lord, because you know that your labor in the Lord is not in vain." (I Corinthians 15:58)

- **Focused.** "Since, then, you have been raised with Christ, set your hearts on things above, where Christ is seated at the right hand of God. Set your minds on things above, not on earthly things. For you died, and your life is now hidden with Christ in God. When Christ, who is your life, appears, then you also will appear with Him in glory." (Colossians 3:1-4)

Christians also ought to be wary of becoming obsessed with dates and times, since Jesus clearly stated that these will not be known to us. (Matthew 24:36) Sometimes various teachers and groups have set themselves up for disappointment and made themselves look foolish in the eyes of the world by setting supposed dates for Christ's return. We must also be careful about becoming too dogmatic about details, allowing them to cause dissension and disputes between believers. Much of this subject is mystery—and will be so until the Lord Himself comes back!

This is most certainly true….

202. **What does the Bible teach about Jesus' return?**

The Bible teaches that:

1. Jesus will visibly return to earth. (Acts 1:11)
2. Jesus will raise the dead. (I Thessalonians 4:16)
3. Jesus will judge the living and the dead according to His word. (Matthew 12:36,37)
4. Jesus will create a new heaven and a new earth. (2 Peter 3:10-13)
5. Jesus will take His children to be with Him forever. (John 14:1-4)
6. Jesus will reign as king forever. (Revelation 11:15)

-Explanation of Luther's Small Catechism

Scripture passages for further study

Christ's second coming: Acts 1:11, Luke 12:39-40; Matthew chapters 24 and 25.

Resurrection: I Corinthians 15:35-56; John 5:28-29.

Millennium: Revelation 20:4-7.

Rapture: I Thessalonians 4:13-18.

For further reading: There are perhaps entire libraries of books written on the subject of the end times, but there are useful sections devoted to the topic in *The Christian Faith* (Kolb); *Systematic Theology* (Grudem); *The Moody Handbook of Theology* (Paul Enns); *Zondervan Handbook of Christian Beliefs* (Alistair McGrath, James Packer); *I Know in Whom I Believe* (Carl F. Wisloff), *Faith and Fellowship* (Dale E. Varberg) *The Portable Seminary* (David Horton), as well as *Four Views of the End Times* (Rose Publishing).

Endnotes:

---

1. Horatius Bonar, "The Night of Weeping: Or, Words for the Suffering Families of God." Originally published by R. Carter & Brothers, 1847. Available as on-line Google eBook.
2. C. S. Lewis, *Mere Christianity* (New York: The Macmillan Company, 1943. Macmillan Paperbacks Edition, 1960), 66.
3. Wayne Grudem, *Systematic Theology, An Introduction to Biblical Doctrine* (Grand Rapids: Zondervan, 1994), 1098-1099.
4. Position Paper: "Teaching About the Last Things. Church of the Lutheran Brethren." Available through ffbooks@clba.org.
5. John Stott, *Living in the End Times* (Downers Grove, IL: InterVarsity Press, 1998), 9.

Chapter 9

Spiritual Formation: Walking the Talk

Spiritual Formation: Walking the Talk

Some years ago I sat in a workshop for women in ministry, sponsored by a seminary in Portland, Oregon. The speaker kept using the phrase, "spiritual formation" - and I was totally lost. Finally risking embarrassment I asked, "So what is spiritual formation?" I was gently told that it is just a new term, more common in the Catholic renewal movement, for a familiar concept—an important concept for every believer to understand and practice.

So what is spiritual formation, and why is it so important?

We used to refer to this as "***discipleship***", and long before that, to "***piety***." The theological term would be "***sanctification***," growing in Christ-likeness. All of the terms refer to the inward spiritual life, which should be growing in knowledge and grace as the believer is nourished by the Word, prayer, communion and fellowship, and which should find its outward evidence in obedience to Christ and witness to the lost.

In our eagerness to avoid living by works or law rather than by God's grace, we sometimes shy away from any discussion of effort and self-discipline in our Christian lives. We can so rebel at legalistic standards and endless "do's and don'ts" imposed from the outside, pressuring us to conform to a group's image of godliness, that we drift to the opposite extreme of license. We may so revel in our freedom in Christ and in His continued grace to cover our sin that we may fail to recognize that we are being given His grace for a purpose:

> "For the **grace of God** that brings salvation has appeared to all men. It **teaches us** to say "No" to ungodliness and worldly passions, and to live self-controlled, upright and godly lives in this present age, while we wait for the blessed hope—the glorious appearing of our great God and Savior, Jesus Christ, who gave himself for us **to redeem us from all wickedness and to purify for himself a people that are his very own, eager to do what is good."** (Titus 2:11-14)
>
> "By the grace of God I am what I am, and his grace to me was not without effect. No, **I worked harder than all of them—yet not I, but the grace of God that was with me."** (I Corinthians 15:10)
>
> [boldface added]

"Now Faith . . . is the art of holding on to things your reason has once accepted, in spite of your changing moods . . . That is why Faith is such a necessary virtue: unless you teach your moods 'where they get off,' you can never be either a sound Christian or even a sound atheist, but just a creature dithering to and fro, with its beliefs really dependent on the weather and the state of its digestion. Consequently one must train the habit of Faith.

The first step is to recognize the fact that your moods change. The next is to make sure that, if you have once accepted Christianity, then some of its main doctrines shall be deliberately held before your mind for some time every day. That is why daily prayers and religious readings and churchgoing are necessary parts of the Christian life. We have to be continually reminded of what we believe. Neither this belief nor any other will automatically remain alive in the mind. It must be fed. And as a matter of fact, if you examined a hundred people who had lost their faith in Christianity, I wonder how many of them would turn out to have been reasoned out of it by honest argument? Do not most people simply drift away?" [1]

-C.S. Lewis

Scripture also instructs us that:

- We have a new Master; we are not our own any longer. Romans 6:18-19 refers to us as "slaves of righteousness," and "Just as you used to offer the parts of your body in slavery to impurity and to ever-increasing wickedness, so now offer them in slavery to righteousness leading to holiness." I Corinthians 6:20 says, "You are not your own; you were bought at a price. Therefore honor God with your body."
- We are told not to be conformed to this world, but to be transformed by "the renewing of our minds . . . " (Romans 12:2)
- We are to "put off your old self, which is being corrupted by its deceitful desires; to be made new in the attitude of your minds; and to put on the new self, created to be like God in true righteousness and holiness." There follows a list of behaviors Christians are to avoid. (Ephesians 4:22-32)
- We are to imitate Christ. "Just as He who called you is holy, so be holy in all you do . . ."(I Peter 1:15)
- We are to follow the Lord. "It is the Lord your God you must follow, and him you must revere. Keep his commands and obey him; serve him and hold fast to him." (Deuteronomy 13:4)
- We are to train and discipline our bodies, focusing ourselves on the prize. (I Corinthians 9:24-27)

We have a committed enemy of our souls whose aim may be to turn us from faith altogether or to make us ineffective servants of Christ by lulling us with complacency, carelessness and indulgence.

So, how do we pursue Christ-likeness?

Prayer—Talking To Your Father

Emma Daniel Gray died on June 8, 2009, at the age of 95. The Washington Post reported that for 24 years she was the woman who cleaned the office of the President of the United States. She served six presidents before she retired in 1979. But, though her task was humble, her calling was great! She was a devout Christian who daily, with her duster in one hand and her other hand on the President's chair, would pray for his blessing, wisdom and safety. Her pastor said of her, "She saw life through the eyes of promise is the way I'd put it. You can always look around and find reasons to be (unhappy)...but you couldn't be around her and not know what she believed." [2]

What is prayer? It is simply talking to your Father. The 16th century theologian Dr. Erik Pontoppidan explained, "To pray is to speak simply (unpretentious and straightforward) with God in one's heart, pour out one's desire for Him, lament one's spiritual need of Him, and from the depths of one's soul seek something from Him." [3]

It has been said that prayer is the most discussed and least practiced of all the Christian disciplines. You have undoubtedly heard hundreds of sermons about it; studied it in small group Bible studies, read shelves of books on the subject, and attempted to keep a prayer journal more than once. But let's remind ourselves about prayer, and then let's just PRAY!

Eight Things We Believe About Prayer

(and you could likely add twenty more to the list!)

1. It is effective. (James 5:16; James 4:2)
2. God invites us to pray and we may use His Name. (Matthew 6:9-13; John 14:13)
3. God promises to hear and answer. (Matthew 7:7)
4. We may go directly to Christ, with no intermediary. (Hebrews 4:14-16) We may even come boldly before Almighty God!
5. We don't demand any thing of Him, and we don't have to be eloquent. (Matthew 6:7)
6. We don't need to hide anything from Him. Psalm 62 invites us to *"pour out our hearts before Him."*
7. We wait for His answer, in His time and His way—with confidence in His love. (Psalm 27;14; Luke 18:1; Colossians 4:2)
8. We may pray continually, as the Spirit of God in our hearts can continually communicate with God. (I Thessalonians 5:17; II Timothy 1:3)

"As is the business of tailors to make clothes and cobblers to make shoes, so it is the business of Christians to pray."
-Martin Luther

Kinds of Prayer

"Do not be anxious about anything, but in everything, by prayer and petition, with thanksgiving, present your requests to God. And the peace of God, which transcends all understanding, will guard your hearts and your minds in Christ Jesus." (Philippians 4:6)

This beloved verse from the writings of Paul tells us much about the content of prayer that pleases our God. Often in our eagerness to get relief in the middle of trial and to be rescued from difficult circumstances, our prayers may become merely a laundry list of requests. We are invited to bring our requests—large and small—to our Father, but prayer includes other things. The acronym "ACTS" is sometimes used to remind us of these things.

Adoration, or praise.

This expresses the attitude that approaches our holy God with an acknowledgement of who He is, and what He has done. We praise Him for His character, His faithfulness, His compassion, His goodness, His love for us….and the list goes on and on. God is pleased to hear the praises of His children! The book of Psalms is often used to help us express ourselves. Psalm 100, 103 and 139 are good places to begin. Lift your face to His and tell Him of your love! (Hebrews 13:15; Ephesians 1:3ff)

Confession

We cannot come into the Lord's presence without a sense of our own sinfulness in light of His awesome holiness. Let the Spirit of God shed His light on you. (Ps. 139:23-24), confess the sin He brings to your awareness, and receive the outpouring of His forgiveness. (I John 1:9). This daily renewal will cleanse your heart before Him and prepare the way for you to bring your requests.

Thanksgiving

This is very similar to adoration, except that it is more specific to you; it is about naming the blessings which He has given—everything from forgiveness and peace, life and health, family and home, to work and pleasures. All of this sweet life comes to us from our heavenly Father. It is often hardest to thank Him for the trials, but remember that these come to us all, they are allowed by God, and they bring about perseverance, character and hope. (Romans 5:3-5) Tell Him how much you love Him for what He has given you and submit to His will for you. The statesman Dag Hammarskjöld, who once led the United Nations, wrote the meaningful phrase: "*For all that has been, thanks. For all that is to be, yes.*" Write it on your heart!

- **Supplication, or "requests"**

There are two kinds of requests– those for yourself, as well as those by which you are "interceding" for others. The Bible is full of examples of intercessory prayer:

Abraham prayed that God would spare Sodom. (Genesis 18)
Samuel prayed for the deliverance of God's people when they confessed their sin. (I Samuel 13:19-25)
Jeremiah prayed for mercy for the sinful people. (Jeremiah 14)
We are encouraged to pray for our leaders and our land. (2 Chronicles 7:14; I Timothy 2:1)
We are to pray for believers. (Ephesians 6:18)
We are to pray for our enemies. (Matthew 5:44)
The prime example of intercessory prayer is Jesus' "High Priestly" prayer for those who believe in Him. (John 17)

10 Prayer Reminders

1. **Privilege:** Prayer is a privilege, not a duty.
2. **Place:** I can pray to God anywhere, at anytime, but I also need a specific *place,* an appointment that I keep, where I will meet the Lord daily.
3. **Presence**: I remember Who is here; Who is listening and seeing me. The Psalmist declares that His "eye is on the righteous; His ear is open to their cries."
4. **Promise:** I know that His presence is accompanied by His promise to hear and answer. He is the Almighty PROMISE KEEPER.
5. **Practice:** A life of prayer does not come naturally. It won't fit into my life without a commitment to practice it.
6. **Plan:** I need a plan for a time and place of prayer. I may need a prayer journal or a prayer list in order to focus my mind and to remember His answers.
7. **Perseverance:** I must not lose heart when answers do not come as quickly as I wish. (Luke 18:1)
8. **Petition/praise**: Remember the balance.
9. **Partnership**: Pray alone with God, but also pray with others. (Matthew 18:19)
10. **Privacy**: Remember to keep the confidences shared in prayer with others.

Remember, too, that Satan wants us powerless, defeated, and apathetic. We must be *determined* and *disciplined* to avoid *distraction* and *discouragement.*

"Come now, little man, put aside your business for awhile, take refuge for a little from your tumultuous thoughts; cast off your cares and let your burdensome distractions wait. Take some leisure for God; rest awhile in Him. Enter into the chamber of your mind. Put out everything except God and whatever helps you to seek Him; close the door and seek Him. Say now to God with all your heart: I seek Thy face, O Lord, Thy face do I seek." [4]

-St. Alselm, 1078 A.D.

Karen Burton Mains, in commenting about three prominent women of faith who had recently died, reminded us, "It is we who must become women of faith and prayer and obedience and service. It is we who must set a spiritual standard for the next generations. It is time for us all to grow up." [5]

Bible Study: Learning and Growing in the Truth

"Not long ago I was across the globe speaking to almost 5,0000 people, most of whom were not interested in what I had to say. This was because I had been asked to give a talk to one audience, but I was presented with a completely different context. About half of the audience was made up of children under twelve, which I was not at all expecting. The audience was completely disengaged with me. Twice I stopped the meeting to pray and ask for silence. I have never before felt so inadequate. In the end, I abandoned the message, read a large passage of Scripture, offered a call to repentance, and then closed in prayer. I came down from the podium wanting to hide my embarrassment. My head hung in defeat. But as I looked up, I found myself lost in a sea of over 1000 faces—young and old—many of whom were in tears as they came to pray at the altar." [6]

-Michael Ramsden

This is the power of the Word at work! It is a reminder that the Bible is not merely words but is a "means of grace," a vehicle through which God speaks and brings His grace to us. If that is so, then certainly we as His followers ought to commit ourselves to read and study it! So how shall we do that?

> "All Scripture is God-breathed and is useful for teaching, rebuking, correcting and training in righteousness, so that the man of God may be thoroughly equipped for every good work." (2 Timothy 3:16-17)

Personal Study

Believers cannot flourish in faith on a diet of weekly sermons. We absolutely must be feeding our souls regularly on the "pure milk of the word." (I Peter 2:2) As with prayer, it requires discipline, time, effort, and a plan. I believe that in these days our enemy has become very successful in diverting believers from study of the Word itself. We often read many books about our faith and stories of people of faith, but they are not substitutes for the Word itself.

Because the Bible is a big book of sixty-six books, and because there are many things that are difficult to understand, we are given many tools to help us in our personal study.

For your toolbox:

1. The textbook is the **Bible.** There are many ***translations***, as well as ***paraphrases*** available to the student. Keep in mind that translations are the most accurate, while paraphrases are useful to increase our understanding. The translation used in this book is the widely-accepted New International Version, but many others are available. Widely-used paraphrases include *The Living Bible* and *The Message*. Study Bibles include many useful outlines, notes, and maps.
2. **Concordance.** A concordance, sometimes included at the back of study Bibles but also as a separate book is a comprehensive list of key words in the text and where they may be found. If you remember a fragment of a verse but do not know its reference, this is your tool.
3. **Maps**. These help you to place locations of events in the Word.
4. **Bible Dictionaries**. These will help you in understanding the true meaning, origin, and shades of meaning of words with which you may be unfamiliar.
5. **Commentaries.** These are notes and articles by Bible scholars and teachers which will help you to understand and apply the text.
6. **Topical Bibles**, such as *Naves* (Moody Press) list thousands of Bible passage by topic, and are a wonderful resource if you want to know all that the Bible says about a particular subject.

See your pastor or church librarian for specific recommended resources.

Group Study

Most churches provide opportunities for study in small groups such as Sunday School classes, Women's/Men's Bible studies, or home Bible studies for couples. In addition many Para-church organizations sponsor small group Bible studies. They are wonderful places to grow together in fellowship and prayer support as well as understanding of the Word. They are also useful in keeping us accountable to study. What is critical, though, is the choice of study materials. Altogether too many Bible study guides are "fluff" - shallow and self-oriented. An entire hour may be taken up in endless talk about what a word "means to me." Or the study may be reduced to neat lists of "How-to's" or to responding to felt needs (money, positive self-image, fulfillment, etc.)

Basic principles of Bible study—personal or group– include these questions:

1. **Observation:** What does the passage actually say?
2. **Interpretation:** What does it mean?
3. **Principalization**: Is there a universal principle here, consistent with the rest of Scripture?
4. **Application:** What does it mean to me? How should I apply it in my life?

Seven Guidelines for Evaluating Bible Study Materials

Adapted from Linda Smookler, "*Thinking Biblically—Evaluating Women's Bible Study Materials*"
First published in the *Treasures of Encouragement* e-magazine [7]

1. ***Is Scripture the authority***?

Are the chapters of the book filled with Scripture? Are the verses taken in context? Is Scripture viewed as the final authority, or are opinion, theories and experience given as much weight as the Word?

2. ***What is the doctrinal perspective***?

Most evangelical publications will show agreement on essential truths of the Gospel, but in other areas there may be important differences. You need to be aware of these differences in view so that you may balance them with the views of your particular theological "stream." This book can help you to do that as you see where Lutherans hold distinct views on issues such as sin, eternal security, election, the sacraments and means of grace, the fallen nature of man, and others. In the Appendix you will find a list of publishers to help you determine their theological "stream", if they are denominational publishers. You should also go online and find the Statement of Faith of either the publisher or the writer. As we have emphasized before, it is not necessary to avoid any teachings on non-essential differences, since honest and godly scholars view them differently, but it is important to understand who you are and why you are, and to be able to support your church's position.

3. ***Does it teach salvation by grace through faith?***

Be very careful to notice if works and effort are made a prerequisite for salvation. Never forget the "solas": by the Word alone, for the glory of God alone, by Christ's work alone; by grace alone, through faith alone.

4. ***Who is the author?***

Go online to find a Statement of Faith by the author, or determine his/her position based on the publisher. Sometimes very subtle heresies can creep into innocent-appearing materials. Watch out!

5. ***Who does the author quote?*** This is another way of determining the theology of the writer.

6. ***Is the book God-centered or man-centered?***
Is the emphasis on how we can be conformed to God's image and glorify Him, or on how we can be happy, fulfilled, satisfied and successful?
7. ***Is the book teachable***, with many helps, and useable in length and difficulty for your group?

Also, seek the advice of your pastor if you have questions about the study you are considering.

Doing God's Will: Following the Leader

"Christian morality is not primarily rules and regulations, but relationships. On the one hand, the more we know and love God, the more we shall want to please Him. We are to develop a spiritual sensitivity toward God, through His Word and Sprit, until in every dilemma it becomes safe and practical to ask ourselves, "Would it please Him?" On the other hand, love for others leads us to serve them. Whatever we wish others would do to us, we shall want to do to them. It is a wonderfully liberating experience when the desire to please God overtakes the desire to please ourselves, and when love for others displaces self-love." [8]

-John Stott.

What do we mean by "God's will?"

God has a sovereign, perfect plan for man—what He foreknows will happen and His actions in our future. Remember that there is no "future" to God, only an eternal present. His ultimate plan for all mankind is that they be reconciled to Him through the death of His Son on their behalf. Other plans for us are unrevealed, but we trust Him because we know His character—we know that He is good. (Proverbs 16:33, 21:1; Daniel 4:35; Romans 11:33-36; Ephesians 1:11)

God has a "general moral will" for all believers to follow. We need not ask Him, because He has made these things very clear to us in His Word. (Romans 2:18; I Thessalonians 4:3, 5:16-18; Ephesians 5:2; Deuteronomy 10:12) Deuteronomy 5:32-33 instructs, "So be careful to do what the Lord your God has commanded you; do not turn aside to the right or to the left. Walk in all the way that the Lord your God has commanded you, so that you may live and prosper and prolong your days in the land that you will possess." Study the Scriptures, and remember that God will never direct a believer to contradict His Word.

God also has an individual will for each of us. Most Christians believe that God has a specific plan for the individual believer's life, ministry and purpose. Some believe that it is only general principles, while others believe it to be more specific. But we do know beyond all doubt that God knows and loves us as individuals and desires for us to follow Him. It would be logical that if He expects us to follow He would reveal His way to us. Most of this clear direction is given as the Spirit of God works through the Word, speaking to us in our hearts.

Can His will be known?

The writers of Scripture clearly asked for it, expected it, and God promised it:

- **Psalm 25:4-5, "***Show me your ways, O Lord, teach me your paths; guide me in your truth and teach me, for you are God my Savior, and my hope is in you all day long."*
- **Psalm 25:12**, *"Who, then, is the man that fears the Lord? He will instruct him in the way chosen for him."*

- **Psalm 143:8-10,** "Let the morning bring me word of your unfailing love, for I have put my trust in you. Show me the way I should go, for to you I lift up my soul. Rescue me from my enemies, O Lord, for I hide myself in you. Teach me to do your will, for you are my God; may your good Spirit lead me on level ground."
- **John 8:12**, "[Jesus] said, 'I am the light of the world. Whoever follows me will never walk in darkness, but will have the light of life.'"
- **Jeremiah 29:11**, "For I know the plans I have for you, declares the Lord, plans to prosper you and not to harm you, plans to give you hope and a future."

How does He lead His children?

He most often uses the Word itself. Seek Him!

He may use circumstances, directing us through the decisions of others.

He may use the advice of others—people who love the Lord, listen to His voice, will pray for us and help us to see what we should do and where we should go.

He may sometimes uses visions, as in the case of Paul's Macedonian call. (Acts. 16:9)

He may direct us to list the options, praying over them, weighing them, and asking God to open and close doors for us.

He may allow us to test Him, as He did with Gideon and his "fleece." (Judges 6:36-40)

He may actually directly speak to us, audibly or inaudibly, in the nighttime or the daytime, as can be testified to by some people of faith who were in particular times of great grief, sorrow and confusion. Remember, however, that He will never direct us to do anything whatsoever that is contrary to the clear teaching of Scripture. Always be careful when you hear someone say, "The Lord told me to do this," since we are easily deceived by our own desires and the enemy himself. Go to the Word!

He may "nudge" us, prompting us by the Spirit's voice to act—to place a call, write a letter of encouragement, or go to our brother or sister to ask forgiveness and make things right. Learn to know Him well so that you may recognize His voice and follow His promptings.

. . . And something else:

- Don't try to apply *isolated Scriptures*, taken literally and out of context, that may not be consistent with all of Scripture.
- Recognize that *God leads in ALL things*, not just the "big ones" like career, marriage, and home. Proverbs 3:5-6, "Trust in the Lord with all your heart and lean not on your own understanding; in **all your ways** [boldface, added] acknowledge him, and he will make your paths straight."
- Be *careful of feelings*. You cannot depend on them. They can be influenced by anything from the weather to your night's sleep. Stand firm on the Word.
- Don't be *immobilized.* Get going! Act on what you know and ask God to stop you if you have misunderstood His leading.
- Remember that God *does not always reveal details.* Noah was not told how many years would pass before the promised flood, but he obeyed God's command to build the ark.
- Don't assume if *trouble* comes that you took the wrong path. Christ didn't promise a smooth trip; just a safe landing. Someone once said, "If you are on a rough road, and you were told it would be rough, it may just confirm that you are on the right road." Remember that Christ Himself—our Guide—had MUCH trouble in His life on earth!
- Check your *own will.* Are you just curious about what God wants of you? Are you looking

for an excuse? *Will you really obey Him?*
- Be careful about *time-tables.* Wait on the Lord for His perfect timing, remembering that His ways are far above ours. (Isaiah 55:8)

So, how can you know and do His will?

By studying His Word, listening for His voice,
remaining in a close, intimate relationship with your Guide,
submitting to His will...and trusting Him, above all.
We trust Him for what we DON'T know because of WHO we DO know!

Personal Witness and Service: Spreading the Word

"*You need only meet one saint to believe, to silence the noisy argument of the world.*"

So said Phillip Yancey of Dr. Paul Brand—the man who became like a spiritual father to this young and troubled young man, helping to restore the face of God in his doubt-ridden world. Listen to Yancey's testimony:

"For years I labored under a huge **apparent** fear: the image of a stern, judgmental God as a sort of cosmic Enforcer. Who would want to pray to that God? With such a fearsome partner, how could I pursue an intimate relationship? My defenses lowered over time as I experienced grace, as I met trustworthy guides, and then supremely as I got to know Jesus.

For a recovering fundamentalist, it takes courage to trust that the gospel truly is good news from a God who is love. I sought out guides who believed this most fundamental and yet seldom-realized fact of faith. For ten years I followed around Dr. Paul Brand, who brought healing and grace to some of the lowest people on the planet, low-caste Hindus afflicted with leprosy. Sometimes we prayed together and always I marveled at his simple faith. He showed a spirit of thanksgiving even as he worked for near-poverty wages in trying conditions. He faced into old age with anticipation, not fear. Even at the end, he saw death as a true homecoming, not an interruption but a culmination*.*" [9]

- Phillip Yancey

Perhaps it seems strange to include ***witness and service*** along with the other disciplines of prayer, Bible study, and following God's will—which are so important in spiritual formation. Actually, witness and service should flow naturally out of a life of intimate relationship with Jesus. Dr. Brand probably did not practice any particular methods of personal witness, any steps to follow to reach someone for Christ. He may never have read books on strategy for spreading the Word (but he certainly may have, as he was an avid student as well as a gifted surgeon). The point, though, is that his inward life with God showed, and that is what pointed young Yancey to Jesus, who radically changed and re-directed his life.

> "*There are five Gospels: Matthew, Mark, Luke, John, and the Christian, and some people will never read the first four.*" [10]
> Gypsy Smith

It is evident that we are saved for a purpose—to bring glory to God and to do His work on earth until He calls us home. Part of that work is to evangelize, to bear witness to the faith within us and to share that Good News with others. Another part of that purpose is to serve Him by showing His love, compassion, justice and care to the world. To avoid that calling is to close ourselves off from what God holds dear; to value the Gospel but keep it only for ourselves. At some point, then, are we not actually de-valuing the Gospel?

There are any number of systems or strategies which may help you as you begin to share your faith with others. Many, like Dr. James Kennedy's "*Evangelism Explosion*," Campus Crusade for Christ's "*The Four Spiritual Laws*," and so-called "friendship evangelism" have been effective. There are also many organizations through which you can reach out with love, compassion, and practical aid to lost people. As you pray and grow in your faith, listen to the Lord's direction, submit to His will, and offer your body—your hands, your feet, your intellect, your skills—to serve others. It is an essential part of growing in Christ-likeness.

For some inspiring true stories of personal witness—dramatic, exciting, bold and true—read Lee Strobel and Mark Mittelberg's recent book, *The Unexpected Adventure, Taking Everyday Risks to Talk With People About Jesus.* [11]

Do you want my hands, Lord, to spend the day helping
The sick and the poor who need them?
Lord, today I give You my hands.
Do You want my feet, Lord, to spend the day visiting
Those who need a friend?
Lord, today I give You my feet.
Do You want my voice, Lord, to spend the day speaking
To all who need Your words of love?
Lord, today I give You my voice.
Do You want my heart, Lord, to spend the day loving
Everyone without exception?
Lord, today I give You my heart.
-Mother Teresa, [12]

Fellowship: Living in Community

The "church" had just been born, on the day of Pentecost.

Now, we are told how they lived, "They devoted themselves to the apostles' teaching and to the fellowship, to the breaking of bread and to prayer. Everyone was filled with awe, and many wonders and miraculous signs were done by the apostles. All the believers were together and had everything in common. Selling their possessions and goods, they gave to anyone as he had need. Every day they continued to meet together in the temple courts. They broke bread in their homes and ate together with glad and sincere hearts, praising God and enjoying the favor of all the people. And the Lord added to their number daily those who were being saved." (Acts 2:42-47)

Teaching, fellowship, the Lord's Supper and Baptism (mentioned in the preceding verse), prayer, miracles, a communal style of life, generosity, worship, praise—and growth. What a description of a growing, healthy body of Christ! Around the world today the church still meets—in homes, in tents, in caves, in great cathedrals and humble wooden sanctuaries, in secret or in freedom. Not all of the activities of the early church may be evident, but it is clear from the Word that believers belong to a body, the Church, of which Christ is head. To ignore the need for fellowship, to forsake the sacrament of the Lord's Supper, to fail to worship Him publicly, and to close one's self off from the teaching of the Word is to begin a downward spiral of spiritual coldness and drought. It is clearly to deny the specific instruction of God through the apostle Paul, "Let us not give up meeting together, as some are in the habit of doing, but let us encourage one another—and all the more as you see the Day approaching." (Hebrews 10:25)

No one can ever say that any church, any particular congregation, or any particular denomination is perfect! To wait for the impossible is to wait forever. Search out a spiritual home where the Word is preached and become an active participant. Do all within your power and by God's grace to live in peace in that community, to support the leaders, exercise your spiritual gifts and promote the Kingdom of God on earth.

For further reading and study: For an extensive and thoughtful discussion of times when that fellowship may be broken, read Dr. Grudem's *Systematic Theology*, pages 873-883. For help when conflict inevitably arises because of fallen people in a fallen world, some wonderful resources are available from Peacemakers Ministries of Billings, Montana. Ken Sande's popular book, *The Peacemaker*, teaches biblical principles of peacemaking, and other resources regarding church discipline and church transformation are available. Reach them at www.HisPeace.org. Another very useful resource is *Becoming Your Favorite Church*, by H.B. London, Jr. and Neil B. Wiseman. (see bibliography)

> "It is God's will, as expressed and seen in Jesus Christ, whenever his people meet together for worship, and whatever their feelings and circumstances may be, that there should be rejoicing in him, praying to him and giving him thanks for his mercies. When a message purports to come from God, we should neither reject nor accept it outright but listen to it, sift it and weigh carefully what is said. In all this, the living out of brotherly and sisterly love in the local church is possible only by the gracious work of God."[13]
>
> -John Stott

Lord of the Church, empower us to

see past myths that blind us,
overlook differences that divide us,
suspect bad ideas that sandpaper us,
intercede for the pastor who leads us,
seek the righteousness You promised us,
so that we may lovingly win those who have lost
their way.
Amen.

- H.B. London

Endnotes:

1. C. S. Lewis, *A Year With C. S. Lewis: Daily Readings from His Classic Works* (New York: HarperCollins, 2003), 286. From his classic book, *Mere Christianity.*
2. Patricia Sullivan, "Christian Lady Cleaned for 6 Presidents" *The Washington Post* (June 21, 2009).
3. Erik Pontopidan, quoted in Carl F. Wisloff, *I Know In Whom I Believe: Studies in Bible Doctrine,* trans. Rev. Karl Stendal (Minneapolis: AFLC Seminary Press, 1983), 97.
4. St.Alselm, 1078 A.D.
5. Karen Burton Mains, *With My Whole Heart* (Portland, OR: Multnomah Press, 1987). Quoted in *Women's Devotional Bible—NIV* (Grand Rapids: Zondervan, 1990), 1377.
6. Michael Ramsden, European director of Ravi Zacharias International Ministries in the United Kingdom. From an online letter titled, "Communicating the Gospel", (October 30, 2008).
7. Adapted from Linda Smookler, "Thinking Biblically—Evaluating Women's Bible Study Materials." First published in the *Treasures of Encouragement* e-magazine; quoted in J. Ligon Duncan and Susan Hunt, *Women's Ministry in the Local Church* (Wheaton, IL: Crossway Books, 2006), 171-172.
8. John Stott, *Living in the End Times* (Downers Grove,IL: InterVarsity Press, 2003), 28.
9. Phillip Yancey, *Grace Notes* (Grand Rapids: Zondervan, 2009), 161.
10. Source of the quotation, widely attributed to Gypsy Smith, is uncertain.
11. Lee Strobel and Mark Mittelberg, *The Unexpected Adventure, Taking Everyday Risks to Talk With People About Jesus* (Grand Rapids: Zondervan, 2009)
12. Mother Teresa in *Life in the Spirit*, quoted in H. B. London, Jr. and Neil B. Wiseman, *Becoming Your Favorite Church* (Ventura, CA: Regal Books, 2002), 122.
13. John Stott, *Living in the End Times*, 43.
14. H. B. London and Neil B. Wiseman, *Becoming Your Favorite Church*, 123.

Chapter 10

A Final Word

A Final Word

During the dreadful Thirty Years' War, German pastor Martin Rinkart had the overwhelmingly difficult task of performing nearly 5,000 funerals of fellow citizens and parishioners in one year alone. These victims of plague, famine and war included his own young wife. Still, one day he sat down and together with his children wrote the following dinner table prayer:

> Now thank we all our God, with heart and hands and voices;
> Who wondrous things hath done, in Whom this world rejoices.
> Who, from our mother's arms, hath led us on our way
> With countless gifts of love, and still is ours today.
>
> O may this bounteous God, through all our life be near us,
> With ever joyful hearts, and blessed peace to cheer us;
> And keep us still in grace, and guide us when perplexed;
> And free us from all ills, in this world and the next.

How is it possible that Pastor Rinkart could even function, and even more than that, that he could praise God with such confidence? It is only possible because he—though weak—could stand firmly on the reality of the true God, and he received grace to thank Him for what remained. His was not so much a body of knowledge as it was a relationship with a Father. *What* he knew in his mind was *Who* he believed in his heart—and from that relationship, praise could still well up, in spite of his difficult circumstances.

It is this wondrous truth—this firm foundation—that sustains believers, generation after generation. At the end of that terrible war, Martin Rinkart's words were sung as a powerful hymn of celebration, with a third verse which he had added:

> All praise and thanks to God the Father now be given;
> The Son and Him Who reigns with Them in highest heaven;
> The one eternal God, Whom earth and heaven adore;
> For thus it was, is now, and shall be evermore.

-story told by Jill Carattini, "*A Weighted Theology*" in "*A Slice of Infinity*" e-newsletter of Ravi Zacharias International Ministries, 2008.

"In the end . . . it is not worldviews, theologies, and other intellectual constructs that matter most to Christians. Abraham is commended for his faith, not for his philosophical sophistication. Noah believed what God said, believed that God would save him, and then did what he was told. But for Christians, thinking itself is only part of what it means to be faithful. At the end of the day, and at the End of Days, what will matter most is not whether Christians have sorted out Christian theology in its wonderful and delicate details: It is whether they will hear this commendation from the Lord in whom they have put their trust: 'Well done, thou good and faithful servant.'" (Matt. 25:21)

-Alistair McGrath in *Zondervan Handbook of Christian Beliefs*, 54.

Let your theology be your doxology...

"O the depth of the riches and wisdom and knowledge of God!
How unsearchable are his judgments and how inscrutable his ways!
For who has known the mind of the Lord, or who has been his counselor?
Or who has given a gift to him that he might be repaid?
For from him and through him and to him are all things.
To him be glory for ever. Amen." (Romans 11:33-36)

Appendix

Appendix 1: Summaries

The following summaries are included here as a quick and ready reference when you are searching for basic information without all the background and explanation. They are extracted from the preceding chapters, where you may go for greater depth.

What is Theology?

Theology basically means the study of God and all His works. The term comes from the Greek *theos*, meaning "God," and *logos*, meaning "word" or "discourse." so we have a "discourse" or study of God."

"Doctrine" is a narrower term. It is what the whole Bible teaches about a particular topic, such as the "doctrine of the Trinity," or the "doctrine of sin."

Essential Truths (pages 10-24)

The Word of God

Evangelical Christians believe that the Word of God is ***inerrant.*** That is, it is totally free from error. It is totally dependable as a foundation for faith in God and for the salvation which He has provided through Jesus Christ. (II Timothy 3:16; I Corinthians 2:13)

> *One thing, and only one thing, is necessary for Christian life, righteousness, and freedom. That one thing is the most holy Word of God, the gospel of Christ.*
>
> Martin Luther

Attributes of God the Father

"Incommunicable" attributes	***"Communicable" attributes***	
Independence	Spirituality	Invisibility
Unchangeableness	Omniscience	Wisdom
Eternity	Truthfulness	Goodness
Omnipresence	Love	Mercy
Unity	Holiness	Peace
	Righteousness	Jealousy
	Wrath	Will
	Freedom	Omnipotence
	Power	Blessedness
	Beauty	Glory

Attributes of Jesus the Son of God

Eternal	Everywhere present	All-knowing
All-powerful	Unchangeable	Self-existent
Creator	Sustainer	Forgiver of sins
Miracle Worker	Head of Church	Intercessor

Eight Essential Truths About Jesus

1. Virgin birth
2. Sinlessness
3. Deity (He is God)
4. Humanity
5. Atoning Death
6. Resurrection
7. Ascension (His return to heaven)
8. Second coming (return to earth)

Attributes of the Holy Spirit

Intellect
Knowledge
Mind
Emotions
Will

He teaches
He testifies
He guides
He convicts
He regenerates
He intercedes
He commands
He comforts

Note: His attributes include all of those listed for the Father and the Son, as He is also truly God.

Gifts of the Holy Spirit

The gifts of the Spirit are listed in Romans 12:6-8; I Cor. 12:8-11, 28; and Eph. 4:11

The Doctrine of the Trinity

1. There is one eternal God and one alone. (Deut. 6:4; John 17:3; I Cor. 8:4)
2. He exists as three persons, Father, Son, and Holy Spirit—each of whom is fully God.

The Church (pages 27-45)

Some ways of grouping churches today

- Evangelical or mainline (primarily on view of the inerrancy of the Word)
- Denominational or non-denominational
- Liturgical or non-liturgical

Inerrancy is the teaching that all Scripture is given by God and is free from error in all its contents.

Purpose of the Church

1. To God it is *worship.*
2. To believers it is *nurture.*
3. To the world it is **evangelism and mercy.**

Three Forms of Church Government

1. Episcopal—Most hierarchal; authority from top down.
2. Presbyterian—More representational than Episcopal.
3. Congregational—The most participation of the lay people of the congregation

Officers in the Church: apostles, elders (sometimes called pastors, overseers, bishops), deacons.

Trends in the 21st Century Church

Seeker-sensitive churches
The "Emergent" church
Decline of denominations
Evangelical Feminism
House churches
Revival of Ancient Worship styles
Missional Theology

Heresies in the Church (pages 48-50)

Why does it matter that I recognize historical heresies?

- **Truth:** The inerrancy of the Bible is at the core of what we believe, and any teaching that discredits or denies or distorts the truth of the Word is dangerous.
- **Repetition:** The same old heresies occur over and over throughout church history. They may appear with a new face, but they are the same old issues.
- **Diversion:** Arguing over and again about what is settled doctrinal truth only distracts the church from its mission to evangelize the world.
- **Destruction:** The enemy of our souls and of the church seeks to destroy God and His people. The ugliness of his face behind much controversy is rarely seen, but he is at work to ruin souls whom Christ died to redeem.

The Protestant Reformation (pages 58-67)

Five major streams of theology after the Reformation

- Lutheran
- Calvinist
- Anabaptist
- Arminian
- Pentecostal/Renewal/Charismatic

The largest Lutheran denominations in America:

The Evangelical Lutheran Church in America (ELCA)
The Lutheran Church—Missouri Synod (LCMS)
The Wisconsin Evangelical Lutheran Synod (WELS)

Other Major Lutheran Denominations in America

American Association of Lutheran Churches (AALC)
Association of Free Lutheran Congregations (AFLC)
Church of the Lutheran Brethren of America (CLBA)
Church of the Lutheran Confession
Lutheran Congregations in Mission for Christ (LCMC)
North American Lutheran Church (formed in 2010)

The Doctrine of Salvation (pages 70-88)

Salvation is necessary. Man cannot save himself.
Salvation is available to all. God's offer must be believed and accepted by faith.
God will not reject anyone who comes to Him in faith.

Comparative Views of Sin

Lutheran	Arminian	Calvinist
Man is a slave to sin, and has no free will. His will is incapable of cooperating with God. Grace enables man to accept the Gospel.	Man is thoroughly infected by sin, but has free will. Man's will is capable of cooperating with God, a benefit of the atonement.	Man is enslaved to sin and has no free will. Man's will is not capable of cooperating with God.
Man is totally depraved.	Depravity is extensive, but could be worse.	Total depravity of man.
Sin is transgression of God's Law.	Sin is a "voluntary transgression of a known law." It is intentional.	Sin is transgression of God's Law.

The Five "solas" of the Reformation:

The Word Alone (*Sola Scriptura*)
For the Glory of God Alone (*Soli Deo Gloria*)
By Christ's Work Alone (*Sola Christo*)
Salvation by Grace Alone (*Sola Gratia*)
Justification by Faith Alone (*Sola Fide*)

Comparative Views of the Atonement

Lutheran	Arminian	Calvinist
Christ died for all.	Christ died for all.	Christ died for the elect. (chosen)
Atonement is not limited to the elect.	Atonement is for all men even those who go lost.	Atonement is for the elect only.

Comparative Views of God's Grace

Lutheran	Arminian	Calvinist
Monergistic: God alone saves.	Synergistic: God and man cooperate in salvation.	Monergistic: God alone saves.
God's grace is resistible.	God's grace is resistible.	God's grace is irresistible

Comparative Views of Election (Predestination)

Lutheran	Arminian	Calvinist
Election is *conditional* on God's foreknowledge of a person's faith. (*see further explanation in endnotes*)	Election is *conditional* on God's foreknowledge of man's cooperation with God's grace.	Election is *unconditional:* based on God's will, or choice.

Comparative Views of Sanctification

What is agreed among most Protestant churches

Stanley N. Gundry states in the introduction to his book, *Five Views on Sanctification:* "First, all agree that the Bible teaches a sanctification that is past, present, and future. It is past because it begins in a position of separation already gained in Christ's completed work. It is present in that it describes a process of cultivating a holy life. And sanctification has a future culmination at the return of Christ, when the effects of sin will be fully removed. Second, all agree that the process of sanctification requires believers to strive to express God's love in their experience. They must devote themselves to the traditional Christian disciplines and daily make the hard choices against evil and for God's ways of righteousness. Finally, all agree that the Bible promises success in this process of struggling against personal sin, through the power of the Holy Spirit."

Lutheran	Arminian	Calvinist
Sanctification is a *process*; one grows in Christ-likeness in faithful obedience to the Word and through the work of God's Spirit in the believer. Perfection is not achieved until heaven.	Entire sanctification is a work of the Spirit subsequent to the new birth by which fully consecrated believers are cleansed of all sin. Sometimes called "sinless perfection." It is *an event* rather than a process. Sin is understood as being *intentional* transgression.	Similar to the Lutheran view. Sanctification is a life-long *process.* Like Lutherans, sin is viewed as transgression against God's law; it may be "commission" (intentionally committing sin) or "omission" (failing to do good).

Comparative Views of Eternal Security

Lutheran	Arminian	Calvinist
Believers can be lost if they fall away or turn from faith.	Believers can be lost if they fall away or turn from faith.	The elect will never be lost; they are eternally secure.
They may return to repentance.	Backsliding is possible; the remedy is repentance and conversion.	Backsliding is possible, but is evidence that the person's salvation was not genuine.

Comparative Views of the Lord's Supper (pages 92-95)

Roman Catholic	Lutheran	Arminian	Calvinist
It is a means of grace.	It is a means of grace.	It is a symbolic/ memorial only.	It is symbolic but more than memorial.
The bread and wine are changed into Jesus' body and blood. (transubstantiation)	The bread and the wine remain truly bread and wine but Christ's body and blood are "in, under, and between" them. (the "Real Presence")	The bread and wine are only symbolic and are unchanged. (Baptist) Jesus is really present and his body and blood are spiritually present in the Lord's Supper. (Methodist)	Christ's body and blood are "spiritually present" in the elements of bread and wine.

The Sacrament of Baptism (pages 96-104)

Three Views of the *Meaning* of Baptism

- ***Initiation***: Baptism is understood as something that God does. It is a sacrament—a means of grace—through which a person is initiated into the family of God.
- ***Identification***: Baptism is an act of profession of faith following repentance and conversion—a symbol of salvation.
- ***Infusion:*** Baptism is seen as "infusing" the believer with the power of the Holy Spirit

Three Views of the *Method* of Baptism:

- ***Pouring***, also called "*affusion.*"
- ***Sprinkling***, also called "*aspersion.*"
- ***Immersion,*** total submersion under the water.

Two Views of the *Recipients* of Baptism:

- Infant Baptism
- "Believers' Baptism"

Comparative Views of Baptism

	Lutheran	Baptist	Reformed/Calvinist
Meaning	It is a means of saving grace (baptismal regeneration.) It is something God does for us by His grace. *Initiation*	It is a symbol of salvation, an outward sign of an inward change. It is done as a testimony of repentance. *Identification*	It is a "sign and seal" of the covenant. It is both the means of *initiation* into the covenant and a *sign* of salvation.
Method	May use any of the three; sprinkling or pouring is used with infants.	Immersion only.	May use any method, but sprinkling or pouring is used with infants.
Recipients	Infants, children and adults. Infants are capable of receiving faith. Faith is actual, not potential. Adults may be baptized upon confession of faith if not previously baptized.	Adults only. Infants are incapable of faith; must reach conscious "age of accountability." Only adults are capable of repentance and faith. Infants are often "dedicated."	Infants, children and adults. Infants are baptized based on the covenant. They are baptized into future faith and repentance.

Last Things: The Return of Christ (page 118-122)

Four Major Views of the End Times

1. ***Amillennialism.*** There will be no literal millennium (1,000-year reign of Christ on the earth). It is symbolic of Christ's reign in the lives of His people throughout the centuries until His second coming.
2. ***Postmillennialism***. Christ will return after the millennium—a period during which the world gradually becomes better and better under the spread of the Gospel. This view was more widely accepted prior to the 20th century with its terrible wars, destruction, and disillusionment with man's ability to improve on human nature.
3. ***Historic Premillennialism***. There will be a literal millennial reign of Christ. It will be ushered in by His second coming to earth. Believers will be on the earth during the tribulation period, usually considered to be seven years. (Revelation 7:14)
4. ***Dispensational Premillennialism.*** There will be a literal millennial reign of Christ upon His return to earth following the Great Tribulation, but believers will have been "raptured" prior to the tribulation.

Spiritual Formation (pages 124-134)

Eight Things We Believe About Prayer

1. It is effective. (James 5:16; James 4:2)
2. God invites us to pray and we may use His Name. (Matthew 6:9-13; John 14:13)
3. God promises to hear and answer. (Matthew 7:7)
4. We may go directly to Christ, with no intermediary. (Hebrews 4:14-16.) We may even come boldly before Almighty God!
5. We don't demand any thing of Him, and we don't have to be eloquent. (Matthew 6:7)
6. We don't need to hide anything from Him. (Psalm 62 invites us to "*pour out our hearts before Him.*")
7. We wait for His answer, in His time and His way—with confidence in His love. (Psalm 27;14; Luke 18:1; Colossians 4:2)
8. We may pray continually, as the Spirit of God in our hearts can continually communicate with God. (I Thessalonians 5:17; II Timothy 1:3)

Bible Study

For your toolbox:

1. The textbook is the **Bible.** There are many ***translations***, as well as ***paraphrases*** available to the stu dent.
2. **Concordance.** A concordance, sometimes included at the back of study Bibles, but also as a separate book, is a comprehensive list of key words in the text and where they may be found. If you remember a fragment of a verse but do not know its reference, this is your tool.
3. **Maps**. These help you to place locations of events in the Word.
4. **Bible Dictionaries**. These will help you in understanding the true meaning, origin, and shades of meaning of words with which you may be unfamiliar.
5. **Commentaries.** These are notes and articles by Bible scholars and teachers which help us to understand and apply the text.
6. **Topical Bibles**, such as Naves (Moody Press) list thousands of Bible passage by topic, and are a wonderful resource if you want to know all that the Bible says about a particular subject.

Basic Principles of Bible Study

1. **Observation:** What does the passage actually say?
2. **Interpretation:** What does it mean?
3. **Principalization**: Is there a universal principle here, consistent with the rest of Scripture?
4. **Application:** What does it mean to me? How should I apply it in my life?

False Teaching Today (pages 51-53)

Six Fundamental non-Christian views of God

1. **Agnosticism** ("I don't know") vs. belief ("I claim to know something")
2. **Atheism** (no gods) vs. theism (some kind of God or gods)
3. **Polytheism** (many gods) vs. monotheism (one God)
4. **Pantheism** (God = everything, and everything = God; God is immanent but not transcendent) vs. theism proper, or supernaturalism (a transcendent God)
5. **Deism** (God is real but remote; he has not revealed himself) vs. revealed theism (God is present and has made himself known);
6. **Unitarianism** (only one person in God), vs. trinitarianism (three persons in God)
   - Peter Kreeft and Ronald K. Tacelli, *Handbook of Christian Apologetics,* p. 252. (see Bibliography)

Contemporary False Teachings

- **"God is Dead"**—God exists, but He is impersonal and uninvolved in the world.
- **Liberation Theology**—Jesus as liberator of the poor and oppressed. Sometimes associated with Marxism and revolutionary activism, especially in Latin America.
- **Universalism**— "All roads lead to heaven."
- **"Oneness Pentecostalism"** - denies the Trinity.
- **Humanism**—The belief that man is basically good from birth.

Let your theology be your doxology....

Appendix 2: People You Should Know

Chapter 11 of Hebrews is widely regarded as the "roll call of faith." Heroes of the Old Testament—Abel, Enoch, Noah, Abraham, Isaac, Jacob, Moses and many others are commended for their acts of faith. There are also the nameless believers who,

"*...through faith conquered kingdoms, administered justice, and gained what was promised; who shut the mouths of lions, quenched the fury of the flames, and escaped the edge of the sword; whose weakness was turned to strength; and who became powerful in battle and routed foreign armies. Women received back their dead, raised to life again. Others were tortured and refused to be released, so that they might gain a better resurrection. Some faced jeers and flogging, while still others were chained and put in prison. They were stoned; they were sawed in two; they were put to death by the sword. They went about in sheepskins and goatskins, destitute, persecuted and mistreated—the world was not worthy of them. They wandered in deserts and mountains, and in caves and holes in the ground. These were all commended for their faith...*" (Hebrews 11:33-39)

The history of the Christian church, from its founding at Pentecost, is populated by thousands and thousands of heroes of faith—from the early church fathers to our generation's world missionaries. Many have suffered for their faith and persevered against great opposition.

Why does it matter that we remember them?

They are role models for the contemporary Christian. Their example of total discipleship, courage, passion for truth and passion for the salvation of the lost motivates us to commit ourselves fully to God. They remind us of the cost of that commitment as well as the faithfulness of their Master who led them and now has given them their eternal reward.

Naturally, this is a selective list and you likely would have included many others—but these are here for your inspiration. They are true heroes of the faith.

12 Church Fathers

Clement, bishop of Rome*
Ignatius, bishop of Antioch*
Polycarp, bishop of Smyrna*
Papias, bishop of Hierapolis*

* *"Apostolic" fathers, who were still alive during the lifetime of the New Testament apostles. Most were martyred.*

Augustine (354-430 A.D.)
Considered greatest theologian between Paul and Luther.
Ambrose of Milan (339-397 A.D.)
Helped lead Augustine to Christ; prominent theologian.
Athanasius (296-373 A.D.)
Great defender of deity of Christ against heresy of Arias.
Irenaeus of Lyon (died 180 A.D.)
Student of Polycarp; prominent theologian.
Justin Martyr (100-165 A.D.)
Greatest apologist, refuted Greek philosophy; author of "Apology."
Tertullian (160-225 A.D.)
Prominent African church father; raised in Carthage.
Origin (185-253 A.D.)
Theologian; wrote many commentaries; student of Clement of Alex.
John Chrysostom (347-407 A.D.) Bishop of Constantinople
Considered greatest expositor; "golden-mouthed preacher."

Ignatius was personally tutored by the Apostle John. When on trial before the emperor Trajan he spoke of having Christ in his heart. The emperor ordered him chained and taken to a Roman stadium to be fed to the wild beasts. Ignatius cried out with joy, "Thank you, Lord, that you have decided to honor me.

6 Reformers

Martin Luther (1483-1546)

German monk who initially sought to reform the Church; founder of the Reformation, posted list of 95 protests against the Roman Church; gifted theologian and teacher. Lutherans are not followers of his, but are followers of Jesus Christ, who used him to point out errors and abuses and who led him to rediscover Biblical truth, especially regarding salvation by faith alone.

Ulrich Zwingli (1484-1531)

Swiss Reformer, who taught the need to have the Bible accessible and understandable to lay people. Greatly influenced the Anabaptist movement. (re-baptism, or believer's baptism rather than infant baptism)

John Calvin (1509-1564)

Influential Swiss Reformer, author of "Institutes of Christian Religion." His theology is summarized in the acronym "TULIP": Total depravity of man, Unconditional election; Limited atonement, Irresistible grace, Preservation of the saints. Stressed the sovereignty of God, and opposed much of Luther's theology.

John Knox (1513-1572)

Leader of the Scottish Reformation. Followers became known as Presbyterians because of their form of church government. Fearless preacher and defender of truth.

Menno Simons (1496-1561)

Anabaptist leader in the Netherlands; founder of the Mennonites.

Jacob Arminius (1560-1609)

Dutch Reformed theologian; came later than other reformers but is well-known for his opposition to all five points of Calvinist doctrine. Stressed man's free will to choose good over evil, conditional election based on God's foreknowledge of who would accept salvation; universal redemption (salvation is provided for all who will receive it); resistible grace; salvation can be lost (he rejected doctrine of eternal security).

Three Stages in the Work of God: impossible, difficult, done

-Hudson Taylor

5 Early Martyrs

The first Christian martyr was Stephen, whose story of bold faith is told in Acts 6-7.

The following five are especially well-known from among the thousands and thousands who have been persecuted and killed for their faith through the centuries including the present day. *Fox's Book of Martyrs* recounts the heroic stories of many. It is said that the 20th century saw greater martyrdom than the combined previous centuries, as believers throughout the world suffered great persecution.

Polycarp, bishop of Smyrna

Early church father; burned at the stake at age 85. A disciple of John.

Ignatius, bishop of Antioch

Church father; thrown to wild beasts for entertainment of crowds.

Chrysostom, bishop of Constantinople

Already in weakened health, was martyred by enforced travel on foot in severe weather.

Jan Hus (1372-1415)

Bohemian reformer; preacher and translator. Burned at the stake.

William Tyndale (1494?-1536)

English reformer and translator of Scripture. Burned at the stake.

Bible Translators and Printers

Jerome (345-420)

Translator of OT and NT into Latin (the "Vulgate"), a process of 22 years; The Vulgate was used by the church for the next 1000 years.

John Wycliffe (1320-1384)

English philosopher, reformer. Believed Scripture should be available to all. Called the "Morning star of the Reformation." Was the inspiration for the Wycliffe Bible, first English Bible.

Johann Gutenberg (1396-1468)

Inventor of printing; printed first Bible in moveable type, making the Word accessible to the masses.

Erasmus (1466-1536)

Published Greek translation of the NT.

Cam Townsend (1896-1982)

Founder of Wycliffe Bible Translators, responsible for hundreds of Bible translations around the world.

20 Prominent World Missionaries—among thousands

The first great missionary of the church was the Apostle Paul, whose three missionary journeys are recounted in Acts.

Patrick (400's)
Evangelized Ireland; in 30 years, most of country was converted to Christianity.

Boniface (700's)
English missionary, "Apostle to the Germans."

Anskar (800's)
"Apostle of the North." Evangelized Sweden.

Francis Xavier (1506-1552)
"Apostle of the Indies" and of Japan; Hundreds of thousands of conversions attributed to his missionary work.

Matteo Ricci (1552-1610)
Evangelized much of China; Dressed as Confucian scholar; successful in reaching many intellectual Chinese for Christ.

William Carey (1761-1834)
With wife, Dorothy, ministered in India. Considered the "father of modern Protestant missions."

Adoniram Judson (1788-1850)
With wife, Ann, evangelized Burma (Myanmar).

David Livingstone (1813-1873)
Opened new frontiers for missions in Africa.

Hudson Taylor (1832-1905)
Founded China Inland Mission; medical missionary who spent his life ministering in China at great personal cost.

George Muller (1805-1898)
Man of great faith; cared for over 10,000 orphans in Britain.

Jonathan Goforth (1859-1936)
Canadian; some consider China's greatest evangelist.

William Grenfell (1865-1940)
Medical missionary to poor fishing communities of Labrador.

Dr. Ida Scudder (1870-1960)
Pioneered rural health care and medical training in India.

Sundar Singh (1889-1929)
Valiant itinerant Indian evangelist in the Himalayas.

C. T. Studd (1860-1931)
Missionary in China, India and Central Africa.

Mary Slessor (1848-1915)
Pioneer Scottish missionary to Africa's Calabar region.

Amy Carmichael (1867-1951)
Irish missionary to India, rescued young girls from prostitution

Betty Greene (1920-1997)
Helped found Missionary Aviation Fellowship (MAP).

Eric Liddell (1902-1945)
Missionary to China; inspired "Chariots of Fire" movie.

Jim Elliott (1927-1956)
Missionary to Auca Indians of Ecuador; martyred along with four others in 1956, igniting new zeal for missions in his generation.

10 Evangelists/Revivalists

Philip J. Spener (1635-1705)
"A Second Luther"; German leader of widespread renewal movement known as "Pietism."

John Wesley (1703-1791)
Revival leader and preacher; founder of Methodism (with brother, Charles); preached 40,000 sermons in lifetime.

Charles Wesley (1707-1788)
Led revivals with brother, John; wrote over 6,000 hymns.

George Whitefield (1714-70)
Anglican evangelist of the Great Awakening in colonial America, 1740's.

Jonathan Edwards (1703-58)
One of America's greatest theologians and preachers; leader in Great Awakening.

Charles Finney (1792-1875)
Evangelist during 2nd Great Awakening in New England, which lasted 30 yrs.

Hans Nilsen Hauge (1771-1824)
Norwegian lay preacher; emphasized need for conversion and godly living.

D. L. Moody (1837-1899)
Great American evangelist and educator.

Billy Sunday
"Baseball preacher" of the 1920's; large stadium rallies.

Billy Graham (1918—)
World evangelist for five decades; counselor to presidents; led largest crusade in history. (1.1 million in Korea)

He is no fool who gives what he cannot keep to gain what he cannot lose. **-Jim Elliot**

Appendix 3: The Creeds of the Christian Faith

The Creeds were written in order to affirm the true teachings of Scripture and to counter the false teachings of the day. Most were relatively short and easy for believers to memorize, especially at a time when the printed word was not accessible and many people were illiterate. The earliest was the Apostles' Creed,[1] which was first called that in A.D. 390 but which is considered to be far older. Legend has it that each of the apostles contributed to it. Other creeds followed, often to address particular heresies that had sprung up.

Why do the Creeds matter?

- They summarize what has been considered through the ages of Christianity to be orthodox truth.
- They help to distinguish what are all the essential doctrines, vital to living faith in the true God.
- They help to identify false teaching. They provide a kind of "template" against which new teachings may be compared and heresy may be revealed.
- The apostle Peter in I Peter 3:15-16 says that believers should "be ready to provide to anyone who asks a defense for the hope that is in you." These summaries of historical Christian belief help you to do that.

The Apostles' Creed, the **Nicene Creed,** (A.D. 325, 381), the **Chalcedonian Creed** (A.D. 451), and the **Athanasian Creed** (4-5th centuries A.D) are the earliest and perhaps best known. Other important creeds and confessions include the following, among many others:

- The Thirty-Nine Articles (1571): Church of England
- Westminster Confession (1643-1646): British Reformed and Presbyterian
- Augsburg Confession (1530) and the Formula of Concord (1576): Lutheran
- New Hampshire Baptist Confession (1833) and Baptist Faith and Message (1925/1963)
- Chicago Statement on Biblical Inerrancy (1978)

The Major Creeds

The Apostles' Creed [2]

I believe in God the Father Almighty, Maker of heaven and earth.

And in Jesus Christ his only Son our Lord; who was conceived by the Holy Spirit, born of the virgin Mary; suffered under Pontius Pilate, was crucified, dead and buried. He descended into hell.* The third day he rose from the dead; he ascended into heaven; and sits at the right hand of God the Father Almighty. From thence he shall come to judge the living and the dead.

I believe in the Holy Spirit; the holy Christian [some read "catholic", meaning "universal"] Church; the communion of saints; the forgiveness of sins; the resurrection of the body; and the life everlasting. Amen.

(**note that this phrase did not occur in the earliest versions of the creed prior to about A.D. 650*)

The Nicene Creed[4] (A.D. 325., revised at Constantinople A.D. 381)

I believe in one God, the Father Almighty, Maker of heaven and earth, and of all things visible and invisible.

And in one Lord Jesus Christ, the only-begotten Son of God, begotten of His Father before all worlds, God of God, Light of Light, very God of very God, begotten, not made, being of one substance with the Father, by whom all things were made; who, for us men and for our salvation came down from heaven and was incarnate by the Holy Spirit of the Virgin Mary, and was made man; and was crucified also for us under Pontius Pilate. He suffered and was buried. And the third day he rose again according to the Scriptures and ascended into heaven, and sits at the right hand of the Father. And he will come again with glory to judge both the living and the dead; whose kingdom will have no end.

And I believe in the Holy Spirit, the Lord and giver of Life; who proceeds from the Father and the Son; who with the Father and the Son together is worshiped and glorified; who spoke by the prophets. And I believe in one Holy Christian and apostolic church, I acknowledge one Baptism for the remission of sins; and I look for the resurrection of the dead, and the life of the world to come. Amen.

"Everything depends upon faith. The person who does not have faith is like someone who has to cross the sea, but is so frightened that he does not trust the ship. And so he stays where he is, and is never saved, because he will not get on board and cross over."[3]

-Martin Luther

The Chalcedonian Creed[5] (A.D. 451)

We, then, following the holy Fathers, all with one consent, teach men to confess one and the same Son, our Lord Jesus Christ, the same perfect in Godhead and also perfect in manhood; truly God and truly man, of a reasonable soul and body; consubstantial with the Father according to the Godhead, and consubstantial with us according to the Manhood; in all things like unto us, without sin; begotten before all ages of the Father according to the Godhead, and in these latter days, for us and for our salvation, born of the Virgin Mary, the Mother of God, according to the Manhood; one and the same Christ, Son, Lord. Only-begotten, to be acknowledged in two natures, inconfusedly, unchangeable, indivisibly, inseparably; the distinction of natures being by no means taken away by the union, but rather the property of each nature being preserved, and concurring in one Person and one Subsistence, not parted or divided into two persons, but one and the same Son, and only begotten, God the Word, the Lord Jesus Christ, as the prophets from the beginning have declared concerning him, and the Lord Jesus Christ himself has taught us, and the Creed of the holy Fathers has handed down to us.

The Athanasian Creed [6] (4th-5th centuries A.D.)

1. Whoever desires to be saved must, above all, hold the catholic faith.
2. Whoever does not keep it whole and undefiled will without doubt perish eternally.
3. And the catholic faith is this,
4. That we worship one God in Trinity and Trinity in Unity, neither confusing the persons nor dividing the substance.
5. For the Father is one person, the Son is another, and the Holy Spirit is another.
6. But the Godhead of the Father and of the Son and of the Holy Spirit is one: the glory equal, the majesty coeternal.
7. Such as the Father is, such is the Son, and such is the Holy Spirit;
8. The Father uncreated, the Son uncreated, the Holy Spirit uncreated;
9. The Father infinite, the Son infinite, the Holy Spirit infinite;
10. The Father eternal, the Son eternal, the Holy Spirit eternal.
11. And yet there are not three Eternals, but one Eternal.
12. Just as there are not three Uncreated or three Infinites, but one Uncreated and one Infinite.
13. In the same way, the Father is almighty, the Son almighty, the Holy Spirit almighty;
14. and yet there are not three Almighties, but one Almighty.
15. So the Father is God, the Son is God, the Holy Spirit is God;
16. and yet there are not three Gods, but one God.
17. So the Father is Lord, the Son is Lord, the Holy Spirit is Lord;
18. And yet there are not three Lords, but one Lord.
19. Just as we are compelled by the Christian truth to acknowledge each distinct person as God and Lord, so also are we prohibited by the catholic religion to say that there are three Gods or Lords.
20. The Father is not made nor created nor begotten by anyone.
21. The Son is neither made nor created, but begotten of the Father alone.
22. The Holy Spirit is of the Father and of the Son, neither made nor created nor begotten, but proceeding.
23. Thus, there is one Father, not three Fathers; one Son, not three Sons; one Holy Spirit, not three Holy Spirits.
24. And in this Trinity none is before or after another; none is greater or less than another;
25. But the whole three persons are coeternal with each other and coequal, so that in all things, as has been stated above, the Trinity in Unity and Unity in Trinity is to be worshiped.
26. Therefore, whoever desires to be saved must think thus about the Trinity.
27. But it is also necessary for everlasting salvation that one faithfully believe the incarnation of our Lord Jesus Christ.
28. Therefore, it is the right faith that we believe and confess that our Lord Jesus Christ, the Son of God, is at the same time both God and man.
29. He is God, begotten from the substance of the Father before all ages; and He is man, born of the substance of His mother in this age:
30. Perfect God and perfect man, composed of a rational soul and human flesh;
31. Equal to the Father in respect to His divinity, less than the Father with respect to His humanity.
32. Although He is God and man, He is not two, but one Christ:
33. One, however, not by the conversion of the divinity into flesh, but by the assumption of the humanity into God.

34. One altogether, not by confusion of substance, but by unity of person.
35. For as the rational soul and flesh is one man, so God and man is one Christ,
36. Who suffered for our salvation, descended into hell, rose again the third day from the dead,
37. ascended into heaven, and is seated at the right hand of the Father, God Almighty, from whence He will come to judge the living and the dead.
38. At His coming all people will rise again with their bodies and give an account concerning their own deeds.
39. And those who have done good will enter into eternal life, and those who have done evil into eternal fire.
40. This is the catholic faith; whoever does not believe it faithfully and firmly cannot be saved.

For further study about the creeds, see Rose Publishing "*Creeds and Heresies*"; Wayne Grudem, *Systematic Theology;* Robert Kolb, *The Christian Faith;* Steven P. Mueller, *Called to Serve* as well as many other sources.
The complete text of *The Chicago Statement on Biblical Inerrancy* of 1978 is included on pages 1203-1207 in Grudem's *Systematic Theology.*

Endnotes:

1. Steven P. Mueller, *Called to Believe, A Brief Introduction to Christian Doctrine* (Eugene,OR: WIPF and Stock, 2006), 288.
2. Ibid., 280-282.
3. Martin Luther, quoted in Alister E. McGrath, gen. ed., *Zondervan Handbook of Christian Beliefs* (Grand Rapids: Zondervan, 2005), 28.
4. Mueller, *Called to Believe*, 282-283.
5. Wayne Grudem, *Systematic Theology, An Introduction to Biblical Doctrine* (Grand Rapids: Zondervan, 1994), 1169-1170.
6. Mueller, *Called to Believe*, 284-286.

Appendix 4: Publishers of Christian Resources

A partial listing of some of the most familiar publishers of Bible Study material with their denominational affiliation, if known; otherwise listed as "evangelical" (*non-denominational, but a Statement of Faith or Beliefs is usually found on their website.*) Many are listed as members on the Evangelical Christian Publishers Association website. (www.ECPA.org), and links to individual publishers can be found there. Their inclusion here is for informational purposes rather than endorsement.

Augsburg – Evangelical Lutheran Church of America
Baker – Evangelical
Banner of Truth - Reformed
Barclay – Quakers (Friends)
Beacon Hill – Church of the Nazarene (book-publishing arm of Nazarene Publishing House)
Bethany House – Evangelical
Bob Jones – Baptist
Bridge/Logos – Charismatic
B & H Publishing Group, formerly Broadman/Holman – Southern Baptist
Charisma House, also called Creation House – Charismatic
Chosen Books, a division of Baker Books - Charismatic
Cokesbury – United Methodist
Concordia – Missouri Synod Lutheran Church
Crossway – Evangelical
David C. Cook – Evangelical (Scripture Press is a division of David C. Cook)
Discovery House – Radio Bible Class, Evangelical
Faith and Fellowship Publishing – Church of the Lutheran Brethren
Gospel Light (Regal) – Evangelical
Gospel Publishing House - Assemblies of God (also TPE Books)
Group Publishing – Evangelical
Harvest House - Evangelical
Herald Press – Mennonite
InterVarsity Press – Evangelical, arm of InterVarsity Christian Fellowship
LifeWay Christian Resources - Southern Baptist (part of B&H Publishing Group)
Moody Publishers - Evangelical
NavPress – Evangelical, arm of The Navigators
Paraclete – Benedictines (Catholic, but publish some non-Catholic books)
Pilgrim – United Church of Christ
Standard – Evangelical
SOLA Publishing - evangelical Lutheran renewal
Tyndale House - Evangelical
Warner Press – Church of God
Waterbrook/Multnomah Publishing Group - Evangelical
Westminster/John Knox Press – Presbyterian (PCUSA)
Zondervan – Evangelical

(Beware: "Watchtower" is Jehovah's Witnesses, a cult. See pages 24 and 51.)

Glossary of Terms

Absolution – Assuring people of the forgiveness of their sins based on the promises of God in Scripture. It is included in the liturgy of some churches.

Adiaphora – Deeds of questionable morality not specifically addressed in Scripture.

Apocrypha—Several books which are included in the canon accepted by the Roman Catholic Church, and upon which some of their traditions are based, but not included in the sixty-six books accepted as authentic by Protestants.

Apologetics – The study of the defense of the faith against intellectual arguments.

Atonement – Christ's death, and how it benefited us.

Baptism – One of two sacraments in Protestant churches (the other, the Lord's Supper) Various Denominations disagree on the meaning of it, the mode of it, and age appropriateness, though all would agree that it is to be practiced.

Baptism of the Holy Spirit – The filling or anointing of the believer by the Holy Spirit, which some Christians believe occurs as a separate event, subsequent to salvation.

Canon - The sixty-six books of the Bible that were determined to be the inspired Word of God. The word literally means "measuring stick", so these writings were examined and tested to meet the standard of authenticity.

Catechism – From the Greek word for instruction. A primer of Christian belief, usually in question and answer form, used to teach children and new converts the foundations of the Christian faith.

Closed/Open Communion – The practice of either allowing or restricting non-members of a congregation's participation in the Lord's Supper. Those practicing "open communion" do so in the belief that all who trust in Christ as their Savior are members of the true body of Christ and should share in the Lord's table, whether or not they are members of a specific congregation.

Dispensationalism – A theological system originating in the 19th century which divides biblical history into seven periods or "dispensations." The nation of Israel and the church are viewed as two separate groups in God's plan, Old Testament prophecies concerning the nation of Israel are to be literally fulfilled, and the pre-tribulation rapture of the church occurs, separate from the later return of Christ.

Doctrine – What the whole Bible teaches about a particular topic, such as the "doctrine of salvation", or the "doctrine of the Holy Spirit."

Ecumenical – A movement to bring Christian churches together in unity and fellowship.

Egalitarian – The view that all functions and roles in the church are open to men and women alike. *Complementarian* refers to the view that men and women are equal in *value* before God but that some governing and teaching roles in the church are reserved for men.

Election (pre-destination)—The belief that the sovereign God has chosen from eternity those who will be saved.

Emergent Church – A current movement of churches using non-traditional methods and practices to bring the Gospel to people. Churches vary in their conformity to orthodox theology and practice.

Eschatology – The study of the Bible's teachings about the events leading up to the return of Jesus.

Evangelical – Churches mostly defined by the view of Scripture as inerrant and infallible and by an emphasis on personal conversion and living faith.

Exegesis – The study and interpretation of a text of Scripture, drawing out its meaning.

Free churches – Independent bodies of believers forming congregations outside of the established state-supported churches of certain countries, such as the Scandinavian countries.

Gifts of the Holy Spirit – All abilities that are empowered by the Holy Spirit and used in any ministry of the church. (see Romans 12:6-8; Eph. 4:11; I Cor. 12:28-30; I Cor. 14)

Glossolalia – Speaking in tongues, using language unknown to the speaker. See the section on the work of the Holy Spirit for various views of the use of this gift in current church practice.

Hermeneutics – The study of Biblical interpretation. Certain rules are applied in order to assure that the true meaning of the text is understood.

Immersion—The mode of baptism in which a person is put completely under the water and then brought back up again. (other modes: sprinkling, pouring)

Indulgences – The corrupt practice of selling forgiveness of sins and release from purgatory, an abuse within the church that ignited passions for reform in the 16th Century.

Inerrancy—The idea that Scripture in the original manuscripts does not affirm anything that is contrary to fact. It is totally without error.

Justification – Right legal standing before God; declared righteous by God because of Jesus' Sacrifice.

Kenosis – Means "emptied" in the Greek, and is used in Philippians 2:7 to describe Christ as he took on human form in order to redeem lost mankind.

Liberation Theology – A theology which places great emphasis on social concerns of poverty and injustice, and which sometimes at its most extreme is associated with Marxism. It became very pervasive in the Latin American countries in the late 20th century.

Lord's Supper (communion) – "The Lord's Supper, instituted by our Lord Jesus Christ, is His true body and blood, in with and under the bread and wine, given to Christians to eat and to drink." (*Explanation of Lutheran' Small Catechism*). Viewed by some evangelicals only as a memorial. The Roman Catholic view is called *transubstantiation.*

Low-church worship – A practice of worship that is non-liturgical and characteristically less formal.

Means of grace – "Vehicles" by which God's grace is brought or "transmitted" to people. Lutherans believe there are three: the Word, Baptism, and the Lord's Supper.

Millinium – The 1000-year reign of Jesus on earth, described in Rev. 20:4-6.

<u>Premillennial</u>: The belief that the millennium is a future event and Jesus will return before (pre-) the millennium.

<u>Amillennial</u>: The millennium is a symbol of Christ's present reign among His people.

<u>Postmillennial</u>: Jesus will return after (post-) the millennium. The millennium is a time in which most of the world submits to Jesus, and peace and justice reign.

Monergism- God working alone in producing salvation. Some assert that in salvation, sinners are completely passive (see the teaching of both Robert Kolb and Steven P. Mueller, whose books are listed in the bibliography, for a more complete discussion of this view.) Thus any use of terms such as "accepting Christ" or "coming to Christ" would be seen as "cooperating in" or "working for" one's own salvation. Many others believe that some degree of response to the invitation of salvation is necessary, otherwise all would be saved, since that is clearly God's will.

Non-denominational—Christian churches or groups which do not have an official membership in a denomination. However, their doctrinal statements, pastors, and practices will usually be closely aligned with particular denominational bodies.

Open question—Doctrinal issues that are not clearly understood because the Word is either silent on them, or our finite minds are unable to grasp what appears to be a paradox.

Open Theism—The doctrinal belief that because man is given free choice, and God cannot know what choices those will be, therefore God does not truly know all future events. The issue is deeply divisive at present, and most evangelicals see it as false, a denial of God's omniscient character.

Paraclete—The word literally means "one who comes alongside," and is used in Scripture in reference to the Holy Spirit.

Paradox—Seemingly contradictory, but still true (for example, the Trinity). Similar to "holding in tension."

Perseverance of the saints (eternal security)—The belief that those who are truly saved will never be lost. They may "backslide," but they will never commit apostasy.

Pietism – The emphasis on godly living as an outgrowth of true faith. The Pietistic Movement began in the seventeenth century as an attempt to reform a Protestantism which had become more of a creed than a life-changing personal relationship with Christ Himself.

Prevenient Grace–The grace of God which is given to sinful people which creates faith. It is described by Dr. Roger Olson as "grace that convicts, calls, illumines and enables." (in his article, "Election is For Everyone" *Christianity Today*, Jan/Feb. 2013, p. 42). The term has varying degrees of acceptance among evangelical groups.

Postmodernism- A worldview characterized by individualism and the valuing of experience over absolute truth. A common phrase that is used is, "That may be true for you, but it is not true for me."

Process Theology – A theology that views God as impersonal and changeable, and that denies what is supernatural and miraculous.

Prosperity Gospel – The belief held by some charismatic groups that "health and wealth" should be experienced by all true believers. Sometimes called, "name it, claim it,"

Purgatory – The Roman Catholic doctrine of a place where the souls of the dead are further purified before being admitted to heaven.

Rapture – The event described in I Thess. 4:15-17, when Jesus Christ returns for his people. Dispensational premillennialists believe that the rapture and the second coming of Jesus are *two separate events*. They place the rapture *before* the great tribulation and the second coming *after* the tribulation. Historic premillennialists, amillennialists, and postmillennialists understand the second coming of Jesus and the event described in I Thessalonians 4:15-17 as the same event.

Reconciliation – The bringing together of two sides. The Bible speaks of God reconciling the lost world of mankind back to Himself through the sacrificial death of His Son.

Regeneration – The experience of being born again by the Holy Spirit of God.

Reincarnation – The belief that the souls of men continue to return to life in different bodies or form after death. It is a Hindu – not a Christian – belief.

Repentance – To turn around; change direction. To truly repent of sin is not only to acknowledge and confess it but to turn away from it, to stop committing it.

Sacrament – "A holy act, instituted by Christ, in which by visible means, He gives and confirms His invisible grace." *(Explanation of Luther's Small Catechism)*
"An outward and visible sign of inward and spiritual grace." (Augustine)

Sanctification – Growth in likeness to Christ. "…the gracious work of the Holy Spirit by which He daily renews me more and more in the image of God through the Word and Sacraments." *(Explanation of Luther's Small Catechism)*

Sinless perfection – The state of being totally free from the practice of sin (also called the "holiness" doctrine or total sanctification). Those who hold this view assert that "sanctified" Christians may make mistakes, but wouldn't define them as sin.

Spiritual formation – The growth in Christ-likeness and Christian maturity that comes by faith in Jesus Christ through the work of the Holy Spirit, and through the practices of spiritual disciplines such as Bible study, prayer, and meditation.

Syncretism – The blurring of differences in essential belief that can lead to false teaching. For example, the commonly-heard phrase: "All roads lead to heaven." Certain denominations use this as a principle of separation from fellowship with other church bodies.

Synergism – The view that salvation comes through the work of God accompanied by man's cooperation, as opposed to *monergism*, which asserts that salvation is only God's work. Man's only capacity is to resist, unless God's grace enables him to respond, or to "cease resisting."

Synoptic Gospels – Greek "to see things together." Applies to the three Gospels of Mathew, Mark, and Luke, which tell of the life of Christ on earth, thus "seeing it together." The fourth Gospel, John, while also relating the life and ministry of Christ, contains much that is unique.

Theology – The study of God and all His works.

Transubstantiation – The Roman Catholic view of the Lord's Supper, in which the bread and the wine in the Eucharist actually become the body and blood of Christ.

Bibliography

Note: *Inclusion in this listing does not imply full agreement with all contents of the resources or other writings of the authors, but they are worthy of thoughtful study.*

Alcorn, Randy. *Heaven*. Carol Stream, Illinois: Tyndale House Publishers, 2004.

Andreasen, Jacob. *Lutherans and Conversion*. 1955. (out of print)

Armstrong, John H. *Understanding Four Views on Baptism*. Grand Rapids: Zondervan, 2007. Counterpoints Church Life Series, Paul E. Engle series editor. Nettles, Pratt, Kolb, Castelein, contributors

Armstrong, John H. *Understanding Four Views on the Lord's Supper*. Grand Rapids: Zondervan, 2007. Moore, Hesselink, Scaer, Baima contributors. Counterpoints Church Life Series, Paul E. Engle, series editor

Ashby, William Brent; Galan, Benjamin. *Baptism*. Torrance, California: Rose Publishing, Inc., 2008.

Bjornstad, James et al. *Christianity, Cults and Religions*. Torrance, California: Rose Publishing, Inc. 1996.

Bonhoeffer, Dietrich. *Prayers From Prison*. Philadelphia: Fortress Press, 1978.

Bowman, Robert M., Jr. *Denominations Comparison*. Torrance, CA: Rose Publishing, Inc. 2003.

Brother Lawrence, *The Practice of the Presence of God*. New Kensington, Pennsylvania: Whitaker House, 1982.

Carbonell, Mels and Ponz, Stanley R. *Personalizing My Faith - Membership and Ministry.* Blue Ridge, Georgia: Uniquely You Resources, 2006.

Carson, D.A., general editor. *Telling the Truth: Evangelizing Postmoderns*. Grand Rapids, Michigan: Zondervan, 2000.

Cross, F. L. and Livingstone, E.A., eds. *Dictionary of the Christian Church.* Peabody, Massachusetts: Hendrickson Publishers, Inc., 2007. Published by arrangement with Oxford University Press.

Deffner, Donald L. *Myth or Faith*? St. Louis, Missouri: Concordia Publishing House, 1995.

Duncan, J. Ligon and Hunt, Susan. *Women's Ministry in the Local Church.* Wheaton, Illinois: Crossway Books, 2006.

Enns, Paul. *The Moody Handbook of Theology*. Chicago: Moody Publishers, 2008.

Galan, Benjamin. *Creeds and Heresies Then and Now*. Torrance, California: Rose Publishing, Inc., 2009.

Geisler, Norman L, *Essential Doctrine Made Easy*. Torrance, California: Rose Publishing, Inc., 2007.

Gjerness, Omar. *Baptism & Related Doctrines*. Fergus Falls, Minnesota: Faith & Fellowship Press, 1982.

Gjerness, Omar. *Knowing Good From Evil: A Study in Ethics*. Fergus Falls, Minnesota: Faith and Fellowship Press, 1985.

Grudem, Wayne, et al. *Are Miraculous Gifts For Today? Four Vie*ws. Grand Rapids: Zondervan, 1996. Counterpoints Series, Stanley N. Gundry, series ed., Gaffin, Saucy, Storms, Oss,. contributors.

Grudem, Wayne. *Systematic Theology, An Introduction to Biblical Doctrine*. Grand Rapids: Zondervan, 1994.

Grudem, Wayne. *Evangelical Feminism and Biblical Truth: An Analysis of More Than 100 Disputed Questions.* Sisters, OR: Multnomah Press, 2004.

Gundry, Stanley N., series editor. *Five Views on Sanctification.* Grand Rapids: Zondervan, 1987. Dieter, Hoekema, Horton, McQuilkin, Walvoord, contributors

Horton, David, ed. *The Portable Seminary.* Bloomington, Minnesota: Bethany House Publishers, 2006.

Hyde, Daniel R. *Welcome to a Reformed Church: Guide for Pilgrims.* Lake Mary, Florida: Reformation House Publishing, a division of Ligonier Ministries, 2010.

Ironside, H.A. *The Eternal Security of the Believer.* New York: L.B. Printing Co, 1934.

Johnson, Benjamin J. *Modes and Meaning of Baptism.* Fergus Falls, Minnesota: Faith and Fellowship Press, 1992. (brochure)

Jones, Timothy Paul. *Four Views of the End Times.* Torrance, CA: Rose Publishing, Inc., 2006.

Jones, Timothy Paul. *Pop Spirituality and the Truth: The Real Secret of a New Earth.* Torrance, California: Rose Publishing, Inc, 2009.

Kolb, Robert. *The Christian Faith.* St. Louis: Concordia Publishing Co, 1993.

Kreeft, Peter and Tacelli, Ronald K. *Handbook of Christian Apologetics.* Downers Grove, Illinois: InterVarsity Press, 1994.

Levang, Joseph H. *Living Lutheran Christianity: A Historical Sketch of Lutheran Pietism.* Fergus Falls, Minnesota: Faith and Fellowship Press. 1991.

Leppien, Patsy A. and Smith, J. Kincaid. *What's Going on Among the Lutherans? A Comparison of Beliefs.* Milwaukee, Wisconsin: Northwestern Publishing House, 1992.

Lewis, C.S. *A Year With C.S. Lewis: Daily Readings from His Classic Works.* New York: HarperCollins, 2003.

London, H.B., Jr., and Wiseman, Neil B. *Becoming Your Favorite Church.* Ventura California: Regal Books, 2002.

Lutzer, Erwin. *The Doctrines That Divide.* Grand Rapids, Michigan: Kregel Publications, 1998.

Maas, Korey. *Justification and Sanctification.* St Louis, Missouri: Concordia Publishing House, 2005.

McFarland, Alex. *Worldviews Comparison.* Torrance, California: Rose Publishing, Inc. 2007.

McGrath, Alister E., general editor. Packer, James I, associate editor. *Zondervan Handbook of Christian Beliefs.* Grand Rapids, Michigan: Zondervan, 2005.

Mead, Frank S.; Hill, Samuel S.; Atwood, Craig D., *Handbook of Denominations in the United States.* 12th Edition. Nashville: Abingdon Press, 2005.

Mears, Henrietta C. *What the Bible is All About.* Glendale, California: Regal Books, 1979.

Melton, J. Gordon, *Nelson's Guide to Denominations.* Nashville: Thomas Nelson, Inc., 2007.

Mueller, John Theodore. *Christian Dogmatics, A Handbook of Doctrinal Theology.* St. Louis: Concordia Publishing House, 1955.

Mueller, Steven P. *Called to Believe, A Brief Introduction to Christian Doctrine.* Eugene, Oregon: WIPF and Stock, 2006.

Pagitt, Doug and Johns, Tony, editors. *An Emergent Manifesto of Hope.* Grand Rapids, Michigan: Baker Books, 2007.

Pfeiffer, Charles F., editor. *The New Combined Bible Dictionary and Concordance.* Grand Rapids, Michigan: Baker Book House, 1996.

Piper, John and Grudem, Wayne. *Recovering Biblical Manhood & Womanhood: A Response to Evangelical Feminism.* Wheaton, Illinois: Crossway Books, 1991.

Pinson, J. Matthew. *Four Views on Eternal Security*. Grand Rapids: Zondervan, 2002. Horton, Geisler, Ashby, Harper, contributors. Counterpoints Series, Stan N. Gundry, series editor

Pontoppidan, Dr. Erik. Warren Olsen and David Rinden, editors. *Explanation of Luther's Small Catechism, 2nd Edition.* Fergus Falls, MN: Faith and Fellowship Press, 1988.

Rottmann, Erik. *One Christ Many Creeds: A Study of Denominations from A Lutheran Perspective.* St. Louis, Missouri: Concordia Publishing House, 2008.

Sande, Ken. *The Peacemaker: A Biblical Guide to Resolving Personal Conflict.* Grand Rapids, Michigan: Baker Books, 1991, 2004.

Sande, Ken. *Transforming Your Church: Cultivating a Culture of Peace.* Billings, Montana: Peacemaker Ministries, 2003. (A booklet in the Culture of Peace Series)

Sartelle, John P. *Infant Baptism: What Christian Parents Should Know.* Phillipsburg, NJ: Presbyterian and Reformed Publishing Company, 1985.

Schaeffer, Francis A. *The Church Before the Watching World.* Downers Grove, Illinois: InterVarsity Press, 1971.

Schaeffer, Francis A. *True Spirituality.* Wheaton, Illinois: Tyndale House, 1971.

Skrade, Kristofer, ed. *The Christian Handbook.* Minneapolis, Minnesota: Augsburg Fortress. 2005.

Stone, Arnold M. *Did the Apostles Practice Infant Baptism*? Fergus Falls, Minnesota: Faith and Fellowship Press, 1983. (brochure)

Strickland, Wayne G. *Five Views on Law and Gospel.* Grand Rapids: Zondervan, 1999. Bahnsen, Kaiser, Moo, Strickland, VanGemeren, contributors. Counterpoints Series, Stanley N. Gundry, series editor

Strobel, Lee and Mittelberg, Mark. *The Unexpected Adventure: Taking Everyday Risks to Talk With People About Jesus.* Grand Rapids, Michigan: Zondervan, 2009.

Stott, John. *Living In the End Times.* Downers Grove, Illinois: InterVarsity Press, 1998.

Sumner, Sarah. *Men and Women in the Church.* Downers Grove, Illinois: InterVarsity Press, 2003.

Unger, Merrill. *Unger's Bible Dictionary.* 3rd ed. Chicago: Moody Press, 1966.

Varberg, Dale E. *Faith and Fellowship: A Look at Lutheran Brethren Theology 1900*-2000. Fergus Falls, Minnesota: Faith and Fellowship Press, 2000.

Wilson, Barbara S. and Flancher, Arlene, *Lutheran Handbook II.* Minneapolis, Minnesota: Augsburg Fortress, 2007.

Wisloff, Carl F. *I Know In Whom I Believe: Studies in Bible Doctrine.* Translated by Rev. Karl Stendal. Minneapolis, Minnesota: AFLC Seminary Press, 1983.

Yancey, Philip. *Grace Notes.* Grand Rapids, Michigan: Zondervan, 2009.

Ysteboe, Timothy. *We Believe: A Commentary on the Statement of Faith.* Fergus Falls, Minnesota: Faith and Fellowship Press, 2009.

Zacharias, Ravi. *Beyond Opinion: Living the Faith We Defend.* Nashville: Thomas Nelson, Inc. 2007.

In addition, the Statements of Faith as well as Core Values Statements from a representative number of denominations have been referenced. Among them:

Church of the Lutheran Brethren of America "*We Believe…Statement of Faith*"
Church of the Nazarene "*Articles of Faith*"
General Council of the Assemblies of God "*Our 16 Fundamental Truths*"
Presbyterian Church in America, "*What We Believe*"
Southern Baptist Convention "*The Baptist Faith and Message*"

Index

Index

Index

Index

Index

Index

Index

Index

Index

Index

CPSIA information can be obtained
at www.ICGtesting.com
Printed in the USA
BVOW07s0045200118
505608BV00003B/5/P

9 781626 972711